The complete traveller s guide

Distributed by:

UK
A.A. Publishing
(A Division of the
Automobile Association)
Fanum House
Basingstroke
Hampshire RG21 2EA

Australia
Gordon & Gotch Ltd,
25-37 Huntingdale Road,
Burwood
Victoria 3125

Tourist Publications

First published and produced
in Australia in 1990 by:

T.P. Books & Print Pty Ltd
Suite 13, 3 Moore Lane
Harbord Village
Harbord NSW 2096

In Association with:

Tourist Publications
6 Pilliou Street
Koliatsou Square
112 55 Athens, Greece

Editorial Directors:	L. Starr
	Y. Skordilis
Author:	Don Sebastian
Typography:	M. Roetman
Design:	C. Mills
Layout:	C. Mills
Photosetting:	Deblaere Typesetting Pty Ltd
Photographs:	Don Sebastian
Maps:	Judy Trim

Printed in Australia

ISBN 1 872163 60 2

Due to the wealth of information available, it has been necessary to be
selective. Sufficient detail is given to allow the visitor to make choices
depending on personal taste, and the information has been carefully
checked. However, errors creep in and changes will occur. We hope you
will forgive the errors and omissions and find this book a helpful companion.

ABOUT THIS GUIDE

Today's visitor to the Soviet Union has the unique opportunity of becaming part of living history. Not since the 'Ten days That Shook The World' have the citizens of the Soviet Union been in the grip of such enormous political and economical changes. The tremendous transformation of ideas and ideology now in progress makes a visit there an exciting experience and gives you the chance to see for yourself the progressive reforms taking effect day by day.

Every visitor loves Moscow and this guide book will tell you why. Read it before you go take it with you and read it again when you return home.

PART I offers a general historical background (including a Chronology) of what is now the Soviet Union and information on its geology, government, flora and fauna, covers all aspects of cultural background and attempts to relate the influences that have shaped the lives of wide diversity of peoples.

PART II delves into the history of Moscow, reveals its sites and sights and even lets you explore the countryside around the Golden City.

PART III, because of the wonders of Intourist, is a rather short list of hotels together with an explanation of the unique situation concerning hotels in the Soviet Union.

PART IV is an A-Z mine of information, including an extensive Shopping Guide, which contains in its own way as much gold as to be found in the treasure houses in the Kremlin.

PART V is a handbook for businessmen that can save fortunes in time and money.

Acknowledgements

Writing this guide meant taking a unique journey through time to relive the history of a truly fabulous city Moscow. Along the way I received help from many people and organizations who deserve credit but want no praise. **Groutas tours** smoothed the way, the **Moscow News** gave much assistance, and my publisher, who helped most by interferring not at all.

To George **'the Pontian Greek'**, goes my eternal gratitude. He showed me behind the scenes, let me draw my own conclusions and proved once again that a friend in need is a friend indeed.

Table of Contents

PART I
General Introduction

MOTHER RUSSIA

THE SOVIET UNION

The inhabitants of Moscow represent a true cross-section of the USSR, its nine million residents daily augment by another three million visitors arriving at Moscow's many bus and train terminals from the 15 Republics that make up this incredible country.

On the streets one sees a remarkable variety of nations because in addition to the ever-increasing number of foreign visitors there are over 100 peoples within the USSR itself who crowd the stores swarm in the streets and rush into the palatial Metro stations.

What they and their visitors see is an enormous city with blocks of skyscrapers and huge monuments along wide streets divided by green parks but united by its subway. Old Moscow was famous for its contrasts of small wooden buildings huddled outside the Kremlin walls or surrounding a monastery with specialized areas where various classes of workers lived, while around them vast mansions surrounded by estate parks and glittering cathedrals were symbols of wealth beyond all imagination.

The new Moscow still has estates (turned into museums) and the cathedrals still have their golden domes and shine in restored glory, but the contrast now is in the new buildings that gleam with their glass panes while around every corner or in the distance can be seen monuments as old as the Kremlin or as new as the space exploration.

In central Moscow all the streets have been straightened and widened. There is a constant stream of traffic which includes many more trucks than usually seen in the center of a major city. Busses taxis and private cars seem never-ending, yet Moscow is the city of the Metro. Without it business would come to a halt. Many who work in the city use first a train and then perhaps several of the many subway lines.

For tourists, shopping is an adventure when it is not done in the special stores which accept hard currency only, for Moscovites shopping is a time-consuming search for essentials. The long lines, the most characteristic feature of a persent-day Moscow life, makes this so.

In spring and summer the many parks and gardens of Moscow are green refuges brilliant with sparkling lakes and beautiful flowers. In winter white hills are covered with the grills of ski tracks and its lakes are marked by the flashing blades of ice skates.

Centre of Modern Moscow

It is impossible to describe either Moscow or the Soviet Union without using a great many superlatives. For example: It is the largest country in the world, its territory extending over eleven time zones. With over twenty million square kilometres stretching from Asia, it comprises one sixth of the world's inhabited land surface. It is almost as large as Africa, twice as large as the United States and three times larger than Australia!

Its borders, 64.000 kms long, touch twelve countries on land and its maritime seaboards include twelve seas belonging to three different oceans, the Artic, the Pacific and the Atlantic.

The Soviet Union boasts two inland seas (the **Caspian Sea** produces Russia's famous black cavier) three million rivers of various sizes including the longest European river, **the Volga**, five hundred lakes, fourteen of which are among the world's largest, **lake Baikel** is the deepest lake in the world, which has a total water volume greater than the Baltic Sea, Russia's border in the West.

This immense territory includes every type of climate from subtropical to Siberian winters of 70 bellow zero and it supports the vast diversity of line naturally found within boundaries.

The Artic tundra is the home of the artic fox, the ptarmigan, the white owl and as the Polar bear, tundra wolf and reindeer forage on land, uncountable flocks of geese, snipe and ducks fish in the lakes during summer. Near the

Polar Circle the tundra gradually disappears into peerless forests of conifers, oak, lime, maple, and birch - the national symbol of Russia-that rise over almost half the land mass of the Soviet Union.

These forests alternate with natural meadows and cultivated areas producing millions of tons each, of rye, wheat, flax, oats maize (corn) and potatoes (more popular than cabbage!).The Siberian forests harbour the incomparable sable and fox for which Russia is so famous. The steppes reach from the Carpathian Mountains to the Black Sea, while the semi-desert zone covers Kazakhstan and Central Asia providing unlimited grazing land to its native fauna.

In the south great deserts offer a rich potential as future irrigation projects transform its arid grey soil to fertile fields and great cities. As a vivid contrast to the Siberian winters the humid areas of the **Transcaucasus** of the Black Sea and the Caspian coastline in winter burst with the flowering of almond, apricot, citrus and tung, while cork trees and the beautiful bamboo shelter native leopards, flamingoes and the prickly porcupine. While on the Black Sea promanades are lined with feathery palms. In this incredible diversity of climes are to be found more than 20.000 plant varities and 100,000 animal species.

The Soviet Union also posseses enormous mineral resources. It is the world's leading gold exporter and while extracting more coal than any other nation, its land and off-shore gas and oil deposits enable it to export these as well.

The Republics

The 'Mother Russia' of lachrymose poets and sorrowing expatriate nobility working as doormen or palying soulful ballats on balalaikas in Parisian cafes is now as much a cliche as 'Father Stalin'.

In fact, although the Russian Soviet Faderative Socialist Republic (RSFSR) is the oldest, the largest, the most populous and the most industrialized republic of the USSR, it is the only one of the 15 Soviet republics which together have a population of nearly 280 million.

With a population of 50 million and an area of 603.000 square kilometres, the **Ukranian Republic** comes second in size to Russia's 17 million square kilometers and population of nearly 138 million people, it provides in addition to industry, an all-important and highly mechanized agricultural base.

The three **Baltic Republics** of **Estonian Latvia** and **Lithuania** were annexed in 1945. The **Byelorussia Republic**, overrun by the Nazis in 1941, became known as the 'partisan republic' because by 1943 60 per cent of its territory was once again under Soviet control. In the **Moldavian Republic** the major industry is food and wine growing, a much appreciated art. In Georgia the Caucasian Mountains dominate two-thirds of its territory but its temperatures vary from the humid and sub-tropical to mountain coolness and it provides all the Soviet states with tea.

Armenia is the smallest of the Soviet Republics but it is also one of the most famous, its capital of **Yerevan** is one of the oldest towns on earth. **Azerbaijan** is rich in oil both from on-shore and off-shore wells, its capital, **Baku**, being the number one oil producer at the beginning of the century.

Kazakhstan with its capital of **Alma Ata** (father of apples) where once political opponets of the Tsar were exiled, has the distinction of having such climatic contrasts that while blizzards are blasting the north, the south is basking under blossoming gardens! **Uzbekistan**, with fabled **Tashkent** as its capital, provides most of Soviet Russia's cotton.

One of the world's great deserts, **Kara Kum**, comprises three fourths of **Turkmenia** but the Kara Kum irrigation Canal makes possible sheep-farming of the world-famous Karakul (Astrakhan) and consquently the manufacture of the beautiful Turkmenian carpets. The Republics of **Kirzhizia** and **Tajikistan** with their mountainous terrain and rich mineral deposits have both industrial manufacturing and a highly developed agricultural and livestock industry.

INFOTIP: The citizens of these republics do not call themeselves 'Soviets', but rather 'Ukranian' or whatever republic from which they come.

One of the many monuments of Lenin

CLIMATE

Moscow can be beautiful any time of year. The cold, which starts in September and lasts until May spring, also brings soft falling snow and glittering ice to skate on in the parks. Mile-long sled races with as many as seven horses to a sleigh- one running ahead with a rider- used to be held on the Moskva River. July and August bring frequent rain showers just long enough to get you wet. But everywhere, whatever the season, are beautiful open skies of Moscow. Unlike most major cities of the world where one sees patches cut by towering buildings, here they can be seen from any vantage point even in the city centre. One corner of Moscow sky might show roiling coils of black and grey while overhead white clouds contrast like snowbanks against sapphire-blue, and in the far distance to the right falling shafts of rain unit heaven and earth.

Moscow's main temperature

	Jan.	Feb.	March	Apr.	May
°F High	14	19	29	43	60
Low	5	8	15	29	42
°C High	-18	-13	-3	11	28
Low	-27	-29	-17	-3	10

	June	July	Aug.	Sept.	Oct.
	67	71	68	56	44
	50	54	51	42	33
	35	39	36	24	12
	18	22	19	10	1

	Nov.	Dec.
	28	17
	21	10
	-4	-15
	-11	-22

GOVERNMENT

The Russian Soviet Federative Socialist Republic is composed of 15 republics containing, for administrative purposes, 20 autonomous republics, 8 autonomous regions and 10 autonomous areas. The USSR has a constitution which has designated the Supreme Soviet of the USSR as the highest authority. This body is divided into two chambers, of equal power - the Soviet of the Union and the Soviet of the Nationalities. There are two further government bodies, the Supreme Soviets of the

Traffic arteries of a great city

constituent and autonomous republics and the Soviets of
the People's Deputies, units which represent the smallest
towns, villages et cetera that altogether form the law of the
land. The first form of government after the Revolution
was the Council of People's Commissars which made the
decision to move the capital back to Moscow during the
night of 10 and 11 March 1918. The Declaration on the
Formation of the Union of Soviet Socialist Republics was
made on 30 December 1922 by the First Congress of
Soviets. Now that reforms are taking place many of the
laws and these bodies are changing.

Moscow University

EDUCATION

In the USSR education begins from the nursery where parents are obliged to start their children in preparation for the following eight years (beggining at six or seven) which is both universal and compulsory schooling. The 9th and 10th grades can be taken either in a general secondary school or in a specialized secondary school such as one which trains students for various professions. Higher institutions are free and can be entered upon passing the required examinations. Universities and all kinds of colleges and academies abound by the hundreds while secondary educational institutions are numbered in the thousands. Those who excel in their studies are given state grants.

It is also possible to attend night school or take correspondance courses which when completed offer degrees. These students who also work are offered many incentives such as extra holidays with pay and may have shorter working hours. There are also innumberable camps and recreational places which offer many educational programmes during the summer months.

The Soviet Union has one of the highest educational standards in the world with millions graduating each year

from colleges and universities, and at least another two million leaving with degrees. All graduates all guranteed work. This high standard of education attracts students from all over the world who come here to study, many partly subsidized by the Soviet government.

COMMERCE AND INDUSTRY

Other than the production of salt which always was a royal monopoly or controlled by estate owners whose holdings contained salt mines, real commerce and industrial production in Russia was started by foreigners during the industrial revolution. With the advent of Communism the state controlled all production and all workers were forced to produce under goals set by party committees.

Moscow was designated as an industrial center and at one time actually had from 12-15 per cent of the total industrial capacity of the Soviet Union. This included food and metal processing, textile and automotive manufacture, printing, publishing and various engineering branches. Under long-range planning most of this industrial base has been removed from the original 350km (220m) zone around Moscow and placed in special industrial areas outside.

MEETING PEOPLE

The first thing one notices about the 'Russian's' is that *'they look just like us'!* This comment, so often made by tourists, especially American, who have many former citizens of the Soviet Union living in the U.S and Canada, makes one wonder just what 'Russian's are supposed to look like! The observation may be naive, but it is true, in clothing from Western shops the Soviets, for the most part, would pass unoticed down an American or Europian street.

The ordinary citizen is also friendly and helpful. Store clerks are said to be far more polite to foreigners than to compatriots. Now one stares when English is heard, and don't worry-the KGB isn't following you! Although it is not the custom for men to take off their hats when meeting either a man or a woman, they do shake hands and they introduce themselves by using both their first and last names. Among themselves Russians also use many diminutives, just like everyone else, but this isn't done except for really close friends.

As in many countries, friends more often meet in public places rather than in houses and for Moscow one of the reasons is the long distances involved. Should you be invited to a private home consider it an honour. One should take along a small bouquet of flowers, not an enormous bunch, or even some ice cream! If you are invited for tea

a few pastries would be welcome as well. Not everyone makes tea in an enormous **samovar**, but rather a small pot of very strong tea is brewed and then poured in small quantities with boiling hot water added to the cup.

If you are invited for dinner you will probably find yourself seated at the dinner table soon after your arrival. Eating is a serious business but the conversation isn't, so no political discussions, please! Don't worry about being dainty with your knife and fork - no one will be watching - but do praise your hostess for her efforts and let your hosts know how much you have enjoyed yourself. If, before leaving for Russia you might be spending an evening in a private home, consider taking along some unpopped pop corn. It might be a delightful novelty and nothing can create a cosy atmosphere more quickly!

Just a few years ago it would not have been possible for a foreigner to be invited into a private home, but now in the new spirit of glasnost Russians are once again gradually learning to delight in their ancient customs of hospitality.

> **INFOTIP:** In general it is not easy to take a new-found friend to your hotel. All hotel guests are given cards which have to shown to the police guards at the entrances. At the present time this is done more for the security of the tourists than for political reasons.

Heroes of the Krasnaya Presnya

HISTORICAL BACKGROUND

The history of Russia, like so many great cities and countries of the world, is closely bound to the flow of her powerful rivers. From the ninth to the twelve centuries Kiev was the center of the Russian soul. There, on the shores of the **Dnieper River** facing the endless grazing lands of the enormous plain which defined a demarkation between Europe and Asia the first Russian peoples began a civilization which eventually would inherit the remains of the most opulent empire the world had ever seen, the glory of Byzantium.

Known as the **Kievan Rus**, this ancient Russian state was composed of lands colonized by eastern Slav tribes on the Eurasian plain. In the mid century the Vikings began a wave of expansion and plunder striking both east and west. They overran the trade routes already established by the East Slavs from the Baltic to the Black Sea and even struck at Constantinople.

Another great city, **Novgorod**, had been established (at one time it was an independent city-state) and it too was eventually ruled by the Vikings. These two cities were then united under **Oleg** (873 - 913) who was so powerful that in 907 he supposedly was able to lead an armada of two thousand ships against Constantinople, gaining not only plunder, but important trade concessions which were to establish bonds lasting until the downfall of the Byzantine Empire.

By 989 **Prince Vladimir** had forced the Russians to accept Christianity over paganism and had acquired bride in the bargain. Under his son, **Prince Yaroslav** (1015 - 1054), Kiev became a rival to Constantinople and the center of both civil and ecclesiastical authority. Its downfall began in 1061 when the **Cuman nomads** began their depravation along the borders and ended in 1169 with the sack of Kiev.

Ghenghis Khan & the Golden Hordes

For hundreds of years small nomadic tribes had followed their grazing herds on the vast steppes. In the twelfth century they were united under the Mongol leader, *Ghenghis Khan*, who for a short time ruled the largest empire the world has seen. The next centuries were a period of relentless warfare and marauding by the **Tatars** who burnt down entire cities and either slaughtering the inhabitants or dragging them off to slavery.

Part of the problem was that the land was divided into tiny warring kingdoms who, when not fighting among themselves, were fighting their Slavic and German neighbours. The grandson of Ghenghis Khan, **Batu** even captured Moscow in 1238, when it was sacked and burned by the Mongol-Tatar tribes known as the *Golden Horde*.

The devasting sweeps of the Golden Horde were followed by their retiring back to their homeland with their plunder and slaves. One entire Russian city of 20.000 was dragged off to be sold in the slave markets of Constantinople. Tribute was then sent to the court of the Khan. In 1480 **Ivan the Great** felt strong enough to refuse payment of the tribute and the two and one-half century span of the Mongolian 'yoke' was finally broken.

19th Century artistry

In the following century many of the great buildings of Moscow where completed, the Kremlin walls finished and the great moat dug around them. They were not able to keep out the forces of the **Crimean Khan, Doviet Gilrey**, however, who in 1571 once again sacked the city and started another of the great fires of Moscow. They were defeated by **Ivan IV** (The Terrible) who had been crowned Tsar in 1547. In 1613 the sixteen year old **Michael Romanov** was chosen by the Russian assembly to succeed to the crown, the first of the Romanov Dynasty which lasted for over 600 years.

The 'Great Embassy'

Peter the Great (1689-1725) whose early reign was first as a co-Tsar with his half brother, **Ivan** and then with their sister **Sophia**, as Regent, was the first Russian ruler to attempt to bring Russia into the western orbit. During these first years Peter had considerable personal freedom and was allowed to pursue his own interests - he was only ten when crowned as a co-Tsar- and he used this time to satisfy an insatiable curiosity which led to many of his later reforms. In 1697 he started on the 'Great Embassy', a tour, supposedly incognito, to England, France and Holland. He brought back many of the ideas which were to forever alter the life of the ordinary Russian and the nobility as well. It was then he learned the skills which would later enable him to launch a ship he had proudly help built with his own hands.

Peter the Great died without a designated heir but his daughter eventually became Empress. It was she who choose the wife of the future Tsar, **Peter III**, the grandson of Peter the Great, a foreigner who became more Russian than Peter himself whom history was to designate **Catherine the Great**.

Patriotic Wars & Struggles of Ideology

Whereas Peter the Great waged constant war with his implacable enemy, Charles XII of Sweden, Catherine waged her wars diplomatically and it was not until the disaster of Napoleon's invasion under her son, **Alexander I** (1801-25) that Russia was once again defending her very existance. When Napoleon invaded on the 12 June 1812 starting the **Great Patriotic War**, it at least had the advantage of uniting the entire country which, by 1825 would have over 800 peasant uprisings.

As a result of these and efforts by members of the nobility to limit autocracy and introduce constitutional government, Alexander II in 1861 was forced to abolish serfdom. In 1893 a young revolutionary by the name of **Vladimir Ulyanov**, with the title of Count, soon to be known as **Lenin**, made his appearance in the Marxist study groups of St. Petersburg.

Although agitation continued the monarchy was still strong and popular, until it lost the war with Japan in 1904. The first World War which began in 1914 was also very unpopular with the Russian people and finally in February 1917 the Tsarist regime was overthrown. After fearful intercine power struggles the Bolshivics took over Moscow and on 12 March 1918 declared it once again the capital, this time of the Russia. Lenin was now in power and he began a series of reforms and issued proclamations which were to change the picture of Russia as none had before. Among these was the confiscation of all private property, everything belonged to the State.

When Lenin died in 1923 another power struggle began and when it was over **Josef Stalin** became dictator. With him began an evil era of terror and repression, especially from the thirties to the fifties. On 22 June 1941 Hitler, despite a mutual non-aggresive pact, launched his **Operation Barbarossa** against the Red Army and plunged Russia into a terrible war which destroyed millions of people and devastated Leningrand (the Venice of the North) with an infamous siege. Stalin died in 1953 and was placed alongside Lenin in the Mausoleum in Red Square until removed by **Nikita Khrushchov** in 1961 and buried outside. In 1964 **Leonid Brezhnev** succeded in a sanguine removal from power of Krushchov and remained until 1982. Brezhnev is chiefly remembered by the Russians for his personal idiosyncrasies (see Humour).

Since 1985 the Soviet Union has been under the leadership of **Mikhael Sergeevich** whose policies of Perestroika now offer the peoples of this great nation the first real hope of a better life. Given enough time, this leader can undo three generations of lost opportunities when the clock was turned back on personal freedom and hope for the future.

The throne of Tsar Boris Godunov

Chronological Table _____

862	Ryrik a Viking (means camp) Grand Prince of the Rus tribe invades northern Russia and founds Novgorod.
897-912	Oleg unites Kiev and Novgorod making Kiev the capital of the first Russian state.
988	Vladimir of Kiev forces Christianity (the Eastern Orthodox Church) on his pagan followers.
1147	First written mention of Moscow.
1156	First wooden walls and fortifications of the Kremlin.
1238	Moscow destroyed by Tatar Batu Khan.
1367	First stone walls of Kremlin built by Prince Dimitry Domskoy.
1380	Victory at Kulikovo by Grand Prince D. Domskoy over Tatars.
1462-1505	Reign of Ivan III who adopted the Byzantine double-headed eagle as a symbol of Muscovy.
1485-95	Present brick walls and towers (with many rennovations) of Kremlin built.

Moscow Sunset

End 15th	The first true Russian state with Moscow as capital Century formalized.
1532	The first stone tent-roofed church (Church of the Ascension in Kolomenskoye) is built in Russia.
1547	Ivan IV (The Terrible) is first to be crowned with title of Tsar.
1555-1561	St. Basil's (Cathedral of the Inter-cession) is built.
1589	First Patriarch of Moscow.
1598-1605	Reign of Boris Godunov.
1605-16-13	Time of Troubles.
1613	Michael Romanov chosen as Tsar, first of a 300 year dynasty.
1620's-80's	Development of the unique Russian architecture brick, white stone and tiles, multi-tiered belfreys tent roofs and towers in one complex of buildings.
1682-89	Sophia Regent.
1698	Peter the Great deposes Sophia.
1700	First cobblestone streets laid in Moscow.
1703	First Russian Newspaper, Vedomosti (Gazette) is published.

1712	Capital transferred to St. Petersburg.
1755	First Russian University opens in Moscow.
1762-96	Reign of Catherine II (the Great).
1812	Napoleon invades Russia, Battle of Borodino, Napoleon flees Moscow.
1816-18-25	The Decembrists, Revolutionaries of the Nobility, active.
1825	Bolshoi (means 'small') Theatre founded.
1830	Moscow gets first general public water supply system.
1851	First trains,St. Petersburg-Moscow.
1861	Serfdom abolished.
1872	First institution for higher education of woman opened.
1895	First celebration of May Day.First tram in Moscow.
1898	The Moscow Art Theatre is founded.
1904-05	War between Russia and Japan.
1905-07	First worker strikes and revolution.
1917 Febr.	Tsar overthrown.

16th-18th Century Carriages

1917 Nov.	Soviets take power in Moscow.
1918	Moscow declared capital of Soviet Russia.
	March 12
1922 dec.	Formation of the Union of the Soviet Socialist Republics approved. Moscow declared capital of the USSR.
1924 Jan.21	Death of Lenin.
1935	First line of Metro in operation.
1937	First Soviet non-stop flight over North Pole, Moscow New York.
1941 June22	Nazis invade.
1945 June24	Victory Parade in Moscow.
1943 Sept.	Moscow celebrates 800th anniversary.
1951-53	First skyscraper in Moscow.
1961 April	Spaceflight and return welcome for Yuri Gagarin, first cosmonaut.
1985 March	M.S Gorbachov USSR Communist Party Chief, beggining of Perestroika and Glasnost.

ARCHITECTURE

All over the world art forms have developed mainly from the materials at hand and this is especially true in the evolution of architecture. The Assyrians and Sumerians used brick, the Egyptians massive blocks of stone, the Greeks marble from their many quarries, and the Russians used wood from their immense forests. With it the Russians began by erecting crude huts with not even a hole in the roof for the smoke to escape, and ended by building magnificent palaces-some to match, or even outshine those of Europe. Then they covered them with stucco to resemble stone!

Many of the museum-estates one sees today are so disguised and as such unrecognizable. This explains why so many of them are closed for such long periods, this impermanent material requiring constant repair. One example. is the Pushkin Museum with its enormous number of rambling rooms, wood on the inside, 'stone' on the outside, now closed for rennovation.

The first Kremlin buildings were all wood and for centuries, repeatedly destroyed by terrible conflagrations, they were still rebuilt with wood. Even the palaces of Peter the Great and Catherine the Great were wooden and, of course, the acres of monasteries were constructed with forests of wood. Using wooden planks for steeples

Typical Stalinesque architecture

Architectural styles on Moscow streets

created the typically Russian 'tent' style known as the shatyor. Two fine examples of this are the **Ivan the Great Bell Tower** in the Kremlin and the **Church of the Ascension** at **Kolomeskoy**. The unique onion domes of Russian churches resulted from early attempts to imitate, in wood, the great domes of Constantinople -.

 Although there is an unmistakable Muskovite style which sets Moscow apart architecturally from Western capitals, the Italian influence is everywhere. This began with Ivan III who summoned Italian architects to his capital to build his Kremlin projects, the Kremlin **Cathedral of the Archangel Michael** (1505-08) immediately reminds one of Venice. Even earlier the construction of the Kremlin walls and towers themselves (1485-95) was supervised by Italians. While 16th century architecture widely used the pyramidal roof style and decorated with tiles and brick-work, the following century demand much more elaborate buildings with many-tiered gables, richly painted mouldings and beautiful tiles with intricate designs.

 In the 17th century the Patriarch Nikon, violently opposed to Peter the Great's reforms, attempted to bring back the Byzantine style but by the end of the century 'Moscow Baroque' came into its own with its typical very elaborate decoration in white stone with red brick walls.

As with art, Russian architecture followed the West. The
' Moscow Baroque' was superceded by the true Baroque
and later the Gothic revival, all dominated and supervised
by westerners, particularly Italian architects. A magnificent
exception is the **Ostankino Palace and Museum of Serf
Art** created entirely by serf architects and artists.

Badge with portrait of Peter the Great

In the middle of the 18th century Russia also adopted
the European taste for Neo-Classism but later turned
inward to a revival of native Russian styles. The best
example of this still exists in the beautiful old building of
the French Embassy. Afterward architecture in Russia
became a collection of whatever was the newest trend-
Historicism, Baroque, and Renaissance revival, Clas-
sicism, Art Noveau and the so-called Constructionism,
which made use of modern technology and materials. The
International Modern style of tiers of glass and concrete
can still be said to be in force. Some of these buildings are
architecturally functional as well as aesthetically pleasing.
The 1980 Olympics inspired a flurry of some not-so-
successful buildings balanced by several very well done
sport complexes.

Stalin had wanted to raze the entire Kremlin and replace
it with the heavy buildings of his era. He did manage to
destroy dozens of irreplacable historical treasures, and his
successors have also torn down much of Moscow's
architectural heritage. But now, at least, common sense is
gradually prevailing and one often sees the facades of
buildings left standing while all behind is devoured by
bulldozers.

Geometrics - domes & blocks

ART

In Moscow one is surrounded by art forms. Public buildings have plaques and sculptures (some most unfortunate) the parks and gardens are filled with sculpture, churches and monasteries contain some of the finest ecclesiastical art in the world, even many of the Metro stations have remarkable statues, tiles, sculptures, mosaics and stained glass.

Russian art while developing its own forms, has always (until the revolution of 1917 when Communistic and Socialist styling and themes were the only art form) followed foreign trends. From the 10th century until the 18th century, painting was confined to ikons, done mainly by monks who created them both as a spiritual release and as an inspiration for the layman. These ikons followed the rigid stylistic forms of Byzantium which severely limited the subject matter and the method of representation. They were not created for beauty, but as an act of pure devotion.

Peter the Great finally broke these conventions by encouraging a western style of painting and he established, in his new capital in St. Petersburg, a school of drawing where foreign artists came to teach Russian painters, he also supported aspiring artists by sending

31

Olympic Village

them abroad for training. Catherine the Great raised this school to the **Academy of Arts** which still flourishes at Universitetskaya Nab number 17 in St. Petersburg, now Leningrand. She also indirectly influenced the cultural standards of Russia, particularly in art, by her acquisitions of entire collections of European art bought at auctions from some of the outstanding collections of the time, buying them for less than one of the paintings would cost today.

In time great Russian artists developed and exchanged ideas and 'schools' of paintings began. By the turn of the twentieth century exhibitions of Russian painters were held in Paris. There the theatre inspired Russian artists who produced brilliant sets, especially for the ballet. The Patriotic paintings of the 19th century in which enormous canvasses depicted Russian scenes deteriorated after the 1917 Revolution into so-called **'Socialist Realism'** in which political themes, meant to inspire the masses, were the only kind of art allowed. Examples of this are still to be seen everywhere, particularly covering large areas of the Lenin Museum.

Another art form not neglected in the 18th century was sculpture, partially inspired by the revival of interest in the ancient Greek buildings and statues which was then taking place on the continent.

During the 18th century a phenomenon peculiar to Russia took place in which serf artists and artisans created for their masters superb art in all its forms. Not only princely palaces, but the estates of immensely rich boyars and merchants (who often owned hundreds of thousands of serfs) were overflowing with their work.

Serf craftsman also created the beautiful marquetry work one sees in the palatial furniture and on the floors of so many of the estates. An off-shoot of architectural design, the art of marquetry was brought to Russia in the early 18th century by European masters who were building palaces in the new capital of St. Petersburg.

In Europe magnificent parquet flooring and marquetry had been created in the last half of the 17th century. The work had been made easily a century before by the appearance of the fine metal-framed fret saw with more than one piece of wood could be cut at a time. In Russia a different and more laborious method was used which resulted in there rarely being any duplication of marquetry pieces. One sees incredible intricate examples of this work in the **Kuskova Estate** and the **Ostonkina Palace Museum**. For those interested, a beautiful book of colour illustrations entitled '*The Art of Marquetry in Eighteenth Century Russia*' can be purchased for only 15 roubles at the Puskin Fine Arts Museum.

LANGUAGE

Russian is the most widely spoken language in the Soviet Union. There are several varieties including '**Great Russian**' and '**White Russian**', but '**Little Russian**' is the language of the vast majority. Its written in the Cyrillic alphabet named after a missionery of that name although as used today it is a simplification of several forms of the alphabet, one of which was devised by Cyrill's fellow apostle, Methodius. The two apostles had created simplified versions of the old Byzantine Greek alphabet so as to enable the pagans they were trying to convert to read biblical texts. In creating this new alphabet they were also to eliminate pagan names which still appear in other Christian calendars, no weekday nor any month is named after a pagan God in the Russian calendar.

There was another major difference between the use of Cyrillic and the Latin alphabets for the purpose of spreading the Christian religion. Whereas the Catholic Church always insisted on using Latin for religious works, the Russian Orthodox Church was able to spread its religion very quickly because it used the local language when proselytizing.

Everyone going to the Soviet Union already knows several Russian words such as, **da, nyet, glasnost, perestroika, troika** and **asphalt** (originally Greek). There are six more one should learn before going. With them, and a smile, you will be able to get through many casual situations without even using a phrasebook.

Spaseeba	- Thank you
Prasteeche	- Excuse me
Zdratrstireete	- How do you do?
Neecheevo	- It was nothing
Harashow	- OK!
Pazhalusta	- Would you mind doing me a favour? or
	- Don't mention it, a very flexible word.

There are many Russian phrase books but one the average tourist will find very useful is, '*Russian for Tourists*', by V.G. Kostomarov and A.A. Leontyev, published by Rusky Yazk Publishers Moscow. It contains charming little drawings, all the basic words and phrases, and best of all, many insights into everyday Russian life. It is worth buying for this alone.

Names

The most common names in Moscow and Russia are Ivanov, Petrov, Scedorov and Kuznetsov, each cames in the hundreds of thousands.

The 'skaya' one so often sees as name ending means 'of'.

V.G.Kostomarov, A.A.Leontyev

RUSSIAN FOR TOURISTS

«Русский язык»

Comrade, (Tavarishch)

To most Westerns 'comrade' is synonymous with communism. In fact, comrade is a simple form of address equivelant to Mr., Mrs., or Miss, It is also abbreviated, to **ТОВ** just as our western forms. The only difference is that 'tavarishch' is used for all three.

LITERATURE

Early Russian literature really began with monks transcribing parts of the bible and other eccesiastical writings in the newly developed Cyrillic Alphabet. The Russian literary medieval masterpiece is the **Primary Chronicle**. It is a saga of the Christian Russians overcoming their pagan neighbours and it was the first source of the beginnings of national pride.

In the same period an epic poem, **'Song of Igor's Campaign'**, continued the heroic tradition. The foundation of modern literary language was laid by Mikhail Lomonosov (1711-65), and carried on by the novelist and historian Nikolay Karamzin (1766-1826), Ivan Krrylov (1768-1844) writer of children's fables, and the romantic poet, Vasily Zhukovsky (1783-1852).

There are many others, honoured by museums, plaques streets, parks and so forth, but the names most famous in the West are Alexander Puskin (1799-1837), whose world famous novel 'Yevgeny (Eugene) Onegin', is still revered by Russians today, Nikolay Gogol (1809-52), Ivan Turgenev (1818-83), Fyodor Dostoyesky (1821-81), Count Leo Tolstoy (1828-1910), Anton Chekhov (1860-1904) and Maxim Gorky (1869-1936). Of course Boris Pasternak (1890-1960) author of Dr. Zhivago, the poets, Yevgeny Vertusheno and Andrey Voznesensky are instantly recognizable as well as Alexander Solzhenitsyn.

Repin Square

Duck pond and ice-skating rink!

THEATRE

Many Russian writers had tremendous success in the theatre including Chekhov and Gorky. Konstantin Stanislavsky (1863-1938) and Vladimir Nemirovich-Danchenko founded the Moscow Arts Theatre in 1898 thereby creating an entirely new art form in the theatre by realistic staging and directing.

MUSIC

Until Peter the Great the church dominated this art form as well as painting and architecture, but Peter brought in Italian musicians as well as architects. The first important Russian composer was Mikhail Glinka whose operas combined Russian folk themes with Western forms. Russian motives also dominated the ballet works of the two most important composers of the 19th century, Pyotr Tchaikovsky (1840-93) and Igor Stravinsky.

BALLET

Wherever Russian ballet appears it is considered the highlight of the musical season and rightfully so. Ballet in Russia had always held a special place in that country's esteem because from the beginning it had been under imperial patronage and was never demeaned by staging as an 'in between-acts' interlude. Ballet had very humble beginnings. It started in 1738 when the **Empress Anna Ivanovna** allowed a small dance school to be opened for children in St. Petersburg.

Moscow saw its first school in 1773. Continued royal patronage encouraged the finest ballet masters and choreographers to maintain the standards which made the Russian ballet world famous.It is ironic that now the opening of the ballet season is attended by glittering bejeweled patrons all over the world, but in its early touring days ballet was performed on sawdust strewn stages for provincial audiences who had never before come into contact with classical music.

After the 1917 Revolution Russian ballet faced the same difficult period as all the art forms and was almost stifled by the unimaginative direction imposed upon it. That Russian ballet survived 40 years of artistic incompetence was gloriously evident in its first triumphal tour of the West in 1956 when the Bolshoi once again regained its crown.

Golden domes & concrete towers

RELIGION

In 1989 Russia celebrated **the Millenium of the Baptism of the Rus**. The Russian Orthodox church is the remnant of Byzantine Christianity through which the Byzantine culture survived after the downfall of Constantinople in 1453.

Christianity came to Russia largely as a matter of politics. Most of the regional territories of the Rus worshipped pagan cults while to the South the Byzantine Empire had a state religion originally brought from Rome but which had, during the centuries, assumed the glittering trappings of exotic oriental cults. It was in the interest of Byzantium to convert the Kievan princes to Christianity first, as a ploy to stop the advance of pagan tribes against the Empire, and second, to draw them into the Byzantine sphere of influence.

In 980 **Vladimir, Grand Duke of Kiev** (980-1015) succeeded his father, and like him, attempted to keep paganism as the official religion. This failed and when the Byzantine Emperor, Basil II, appealed to Vladimir for help against the renegade general, Bardas Phocas, an agreement was struck between the two. Vladimir agreed to send 6.000 troops to defend the Emperor and in return the '**Tsar of all the Russias**' was to be given the Emperor's sister, **Anna**, as a bride (this honour was a great political coup which would solidify Vladimiri's right to rule over all the Rus territories) and Vladimir agreed to convert his followers to Christianity. Vladimir himself was baptised 1n 989 and received the Christian name, **Vasily**, in honour of the Emperor's patron, St. Basil. The new religion was forced upon Vasili's reluctant subjects and Constantinople sent a Metropolitan to organize Russia as part of the Partiarchate of Constantinople, both parties had won tremendous advantages.

When the Roman Empire was divided in 395 with the Western capital remaining in Rome and an Eastern capital established at Constantinople, the Christian Church remained united with the Pope in Rome having supreme authority over his subordinate, the Patriarch of Constantnople. Before long the Eastern and Western branches were at odds not only over questions of authority but also on issues such as the use of leavened or unleavend bread in celebration of the Eucharist. The final breach came in 1054 (the breach was not healed until 1965 when Pope Paul VI and Patriarch Athanagoras formally removed the excommunication of 1054). By this time Eastern Orthodoxy had separate patriarchal thrones in Alexandria, Antioch and Jerusalem as well as Constantinople and Moscow. Supreme authority rested in Constantinople and it so remained until Peter the Great declared the Russia Church no longer under the Patriarch of Constantinople and place it under the administration of the **Holy Governing Synod**.

With the Bolshiviks in power after the 1917 Revolution the Russian Church began a very stormy period. By this time it had 68 dioceses nearly 54.000 churches and over 23.000 chapels and prayer houses claiming a following of 120 million. The Patriarchate was restored in 1918 and it continued to resist the Socialist Revolution by every power within its means. In 1921 there was a severe famine due to drought and Lenin, who had already confiscated church property, now ordered that all church valuables-diamond studded ikons, silver shrines (the shrine of St. Alexandre of the Svir containing his relics weighed 327 kilos) and other church paraphenalia which had accumulated over the centuries be collected and sold to aid the famine victims. His rationale was that all this now was 'the property of the people'. **Patriarch Tikhon** responded by declaring such requisitioning to be an act of sacrilege.

This infuriated the regime since previously the Church had made donations in time of emergency during both the Russo-Japanese and the First World War. The Patriarch was first placed under house arrest and then tried along with thousands others of the clergy.

Eventually several church organizations were formed and Patriarch Tikhon was deposed. The State declared that Atheism 'did irreparable damage to the Russian Orthodox Church'. This statement appeared as late as 1988, and yet, despite Stalin, who pulled down the crosses from the steeples, the Nazis, and all that has happened since, the glory of Russian Orthodoxy remains.

The crosses that Stalin cut from the steeples have since been replaced. In Russia they are always seen on top of a crescent and there are two explanations given for the two being together. One, and propably the true one, is that the crescent shape is actually an anchor and as such a symbol of hope and stability for the Christian religion. Others claim that this juxposition of the cross over the crescent symbolizes the triumph of Christianity over Islam.

Skylines of Moscow

The Calendar

When Byzantium fell in 1453 Russia preserved its calendar as well as its Christianity. The first attempt to bring an accurate calendar to the West (important because accurate planting times were needed for the corps) was made by Julius Caesar in 45 B.C. when he gave the **Julian Calendar** to the Romans.

This calendar, brought to Constantinople from Rome, was used until 1582 when Pope Gregory XIII introduced the **Georgian Calendar** because over the centuries a serious difference between this and the astronomical calendar had developed. Pope Gregory's Calculations were based on his belief that the world had been created on 1 September 5509 B.C. Therefore, when Peter the Great returned to Russia from his 'Great Embassy' to the West in 1698, the Russians were celebrating New Year's as the 1 September 7206. This seemed perfectly logical to them because they believed that the earth would have been created in the fall when man could gather the harvest rather than in the winter when he would surely starve.

But Peter was adamant that among his reforms Russia would adopt the **Western Calendar**. Thus, New Year became January the 1st 1700. However, in 1752, when even England had accepted the **Gregorian Calendar** (Protestant countries resisted a 'Popish calendar) Russia still kept to the Byzantine calendar which, by the twentieth century was thirteen days out of step with the rest of the world. After the Soviets took power in 1918 they adopted the western calendar, this made the 25th October Revolution celebrations take place on 7th November.

Old Moscow Mansion

THE ECONOMY

According to one book published in the Soviet Union as late as 1985 *'the Soviet planned economy is free from crisis..'* This same book goes on to explain that the economy *'is effected by a series of five-year plans..'* eventually submitted to *'all ministries and departments, republican councils of ministers, USSR Academy of Sciences and other organizations have their say. Subsequently, work on the plan continues on USSR Supreme Soviet committes, and only after that is the Law on the Five-Year Plan ratified by the Soviet parliament'*.

Citizens of the Soviet Union today are inextricably enmeshed in the coils of a three-headed economy **Hydra** which not only makes their lives difficult, but also threatens the ability of the present government to carry out its stated policies. All three heads grew from the Communist body which is now trying to slip its skin and through Perestroika (meaning to rebuilt) grow a new economy.

The greatest evil is the bureaucracy which, with its endless forums, groups, committees and layered bureaucrats prevents either a quick or permanent decision. Because of this permission to launch even the most straight-forward business project can take years of ceaseless effort with no quarantee that a 'Da' today may not mean a 'Nyet' tomorrow.

As a result of this gross inefficiency the second head of the Hydra causing misery in everyman's life is the lack of consumer goods. With the Hydra's constricting coils relaxing somewhat allowing a certain amount of enterprise and co-op production a few shortages are slowly easing. The fact that long lines exist for almost every necessity prove how painfully slow the process is moving.

The third head of the Hydra has the proverbial double horns of dilema-lack of hard currency and the inconvertability of the rouble. Because of this even companies willing to chalenge the bastions of Soviet bureaucracy fall to wayside, their lances dulled on the impenetrable armour of the rouble, a currency with no value outside the Soviet Union.

The magazine Time reported the experience of one farmer from the USA who went to work on a **kolkhoz** (collective farm) as part of an excange programme. He discovered that there was a supervisor for every 24 workers and that 146 workers were required to farm the same acreage that 4 members of his family caltivated back home. This 'assembly line mentality' has produce a national apathy which must also be overcome once the incentives of private gain replace the restrictions of State Monopoly.

Now that Mikhail S. Gorbachev has purged most of the ancient regime he is in a better position to carry out the reforms which are necessary to save the Soviet Economy which, at 14 per cent of the GNP is far more devastating that even the horrendous trillion dollar debt of the USA. A turn-around of the economy is imperitive for his survival as well as that of the Soviet Union.

Some Westerners don't understand why, in view of the tremendous changes in their country, freedoms not dreamed of before, that the popularity of Mr. Gorbachev is not overwhelming. The fact is that until the lines get shorter and consumer choice gets greater the general population will remain unenthusiastic. Until the stores are full, his hopes remain empty. The fact that the best economy in the Soviet Union is the underground economy is best illustrated by the current saying: '*The shops are empty but the houses are full*'.

HUMOUR

The 'melancholy' Russian is not an entirely true picture of these people who enjoy humour as much as anyone else, although it can sometimes be dark humour:
'Petrov, drowing his sorrows in the local 'Pivnaja' (bar) wanders outside and goes through Alexandrovsky Garden to the Grave of the Unknown Soldier. Standing in front of the monument Petrov says, 'Good evening, how are you? back comes the answer, 'Sehr gut, danke!'

Concerning aspects of everyday life:
'During the Month of Good Service a man went into a butcher shop where the woman behind the counter was notorious for her bad temper. He demanded to see a cut of meat lying in the showcase, and then another and another, knowing very well the clerk dared not vent her anger at him. Growing more and more agitated, afraid to tell the customer what she thought, she finally burst out with 'You keep on looking and I will go to Hell!'

A favourite target of Russian satire was Leonid Brezhnev a very stolid man who mumbled in his speeches and never uttered a word not already written down for him:
'One day Brezhnev was alone in his apartment and someone knocked on the door. He rushed to his desk and started rummaging through the drawers. The knock came again, and still no answer.Frantically searching, Brezhnev

finally found the piece of paper he was looking for. Harrying to the door, he read. Who is there?'

One of the best jokes about him concerned his love of wearing medals. It was rumoured that he had an operation to make his chest wider to make more room for them! The Russians laughed about his affection for medals and came up with this:

One day Brezhev, who knew what people were saying about him behind his back, flew into a rage and called a press conference. 'You are always saying that I wear too many medals and I am always trying to get new ones. I'm telling you now this isn't true! I just came back from that wonderful Socialist country in Africa, Mau Mau, and they gave me the highest order of their glorious country, The Grand Order of the Freedom of the People, the Golden Nose Ring. But as you see, I am not wearing it!'

Cosmos Pavillion

PART II
Sightseeing

опъщаолепвжесопвпвблгчыс
пвпоудемоу . гакодасопиорн
рсвысаменіемвсоспаоленоу .
апрупыаолчцанашлавца . н

MOSCOW

THROUGH THE CENTURIES

The capital of the USSR, on the banks of the **Moskva River** from where it got its name, is almost in the exact geopraphical centre of European Russia. Archeological evidence shows that crude settlements had been here for five thousand years and that even a small wooden fort had been built to protect the inhabitants from marauders sweeping up and down the river. Moscow was first mentioned in the chronicles of 1147 when the ambitious **Prince Yuri** (the Long-Armed) of Suzdal arranged a meeting here with his relative and ally, **Prince Svyatoslov**. Prince Yuri planned to extend his territories by capturing the Principality of **Kiev**, a powerful state whose capital was so rich that its churches competed in their magnificence with those of Constantinople.

This meeting-cum-banquet was a diplomatic maneuver to protect his rear, so to speak, and two years later he made his move and captured Kiev. Perhaps the downfall of Kiev reminded Prince Yuri of the strategic importance of that little settlement on the Moskva at the junction of the Moskva and **Neglinnaya** (now channeled underground) Rivers near other waterways leading to the **Volga** in the North and the **Oka River** to the South. In 1156 he ordered that a strong wooden 'kreml', or fortress, be built there at the highest elevation along the bank.

Overthrow of Mongol Hordes

Over the next two centuries all the provinces of the **Rus** were invaded and conquered by the Mongol-Tatar armies of Ghengin Khan and later the Golden Horde of his grandson, Batu Khan. Thereafter Russian princes kept their lands and titles only by paying tribute to these Mongol Khans.

One of these, **Ivan I Danilovich** (1325-40), was so good at collecting taxes for his overlords that he was nicknamed 'Kalita' moneybags, and was rewarded for his zeal by being appointed **Grand Prince**. In 1339 Prince Ivan used part of the tax money to built oaken walls around what had by now become larger Moscow despite it been razed by the Mongols in 1238.

These were replaced in 1367 by **Prince Dmitry Donskoy** who erected the first stone walls of the Kremlin. In 1380 Prince Donskoy (see Monastaries) fought the

Battle of Kulikovo Field and completely routed the Tatars, giving the Golden Horde their first defeat by Russian forces. Two years later the Mongols were back and once again completely burnt and razed the city of Moscow. Not until 1480 under Ivan III (1462-1505) was their power broken forever, Moscow was finally free to follow its destiny.

Cathederal of the Assumption

Beginning of the Russian Orthodoxy

Constantinople had fallen in 1453 and all the pomp and circumstance of the Orthodox Church had been trans-ferred to Moscow, now declared the Third Rome (there was never to be another) and the Russian Church considered it self to be the only legitimate heir and torch-bearer of the 'true religion'. **Ivan III**, until now only the Grand Prince of Moscow, proclaimed himself Tsar of All the Russias and adopted the trappings of Byzantine power, inclicing the imperial double-headed eagle. He also sought legitimacy for his throne by marrying the niece of the ill-fated last Emperor of Byzantium, *'the exceeding ugly Sophia Paleogus'* whose vast bulk broke down the imperial bed.

Moscow was now the centre of both civil and ecclesiastical power and under Ivan III became the first capital of a centralized Russia State. Its first stone palaces were erected in 1450-1470, the **Cathedral of the Assumption** was completed in 1479, in 1484 the **Cathedral of the Annunciation** was began and one year later the brick walls and twenty towers of the Kremlin were started.

Tsars before Peter the Great

In 1547 **Ivan IV**, grandson of Ivan III, was officially crowned as Tsar, a title which remained until the downfall of the **Romanov Dynasty** in 1917. In the same year Moscow was engulfed, despite its many new buildings, in yet another great conflagration which actually was beneficial in that it made way for even more glorious structures, including St. Basil's and the Ivan the Great Bell Tower, erected in celebration of victory over the **Kazan Khanate**.

When Ivan IV (known as Ivan Terrible although in Russia the epithet Groznyi, means 'awe-inspiring') died, his eldest surviving son, **Feodori** took over the throne, but it was a reign in name only since the real power was taken by **Boris Godunov** whose sister was the wife of Feodor. When Feodor died in 1598 the National Assembly elected Boris as Tsar and although he was an effective ruler rumours that he had murdered his only rival, **Prince Dmitri**, **Ivan the Terrible's** youngest son, were to overshadow his reign.

After the death of Boris in 1605 came the Time of the Troubles when the Kremlin was captured and Moscow was occupied by the Poles until 1612 when the patriots, **Kuzma Minin** and **Dmitry Pozharsky** rallied what was basically a home guard and drove the invaders out. In the following year the 17 year old **Michael Romanov** was elected Tsar, the beginning of a 600 year dynasty.

Red Stars over Moscow

In the meantime Moscow had seen three Dmitrys, all claiming to be the missing Dmitry supposedly murdered by Boris Godunov. This bizarre episode of history was highlighted by the capture of one who was promptly killed, cremated and his ashes shot from a cannon toward Poland, the direction from which he had come!

When Michael died his son **Alexis** became Tsar in 1645, his death brought **Feodor III** to the throne but when he died in 1682 a power struggle began between **Sophia** and **Peter**, both children of Alexis, but by different wives. The heir to the throne was actually **Ivan**, Peter's half brother, but Ivan was physically weak and mentally retarded. The National Assembly chose Peter over Ivan. Sophia Ivan's sister and Peter's half sister, had rumours spread that Peter intended having Ivan and that entire side of the royal family murdered. This inflamed the **Streltsy** who were the professional pikesman and musketeers assigned to protecting the Kremlin and the royal family.

Three days of atrocious rampage ensued when Peter saw most of his mother's family murdered (thus influencing his rule the rest of his life) and order was finally restored. Sophia had managed to have Ivan declared co-Tsar with Peter, herself as Regent. Not content with this (she had a portrait painted with herself in full imperial regalia) she had her supporters agitate for her to became Tsarina. In the ensuing struggle she was outmaneuvered by Peter who finally forced her to enter the **Novodevichiy Convent**, from where she once again made an unsuccessful bid for the throne.

Peter the Great

Peter had an insatiable curiosity combined with the firm conviction that Russia's salvation lie in assimilating the knowledge of the West. He was also determined that Russia would become a great naval power although at the time Russia possessed not one ship nor a ship port, precepts which were to dominate his entire reign and in the end earn him, by declaration of the National Assembly, the title, '**Peter the Great**'.

On the 16 May 1703, on the Gulf of Finland at the delta of the **Neva** (meaning mud) River, Peter dug the first shovel of sod which began the incredible project of turning a vast swampland into the magnificent St. Petersburg, his new capital, 'the Venice of the North', and the realization of his dreams of a Russia equal with the West in trading and sea power.

St. Petersburg was never officially proclaimed the capital of Russia, but Peter forced the nobility and the powerful merchants to build palaces in his new city. Although Moscow was no longer the administrative center of Russia, it remained the soul of Russia and when it was captured by Napoleon in 1812, all Russia was devastated. It was not until 1918 that Moscow once again regained her title, but now she became not only the capital of Russia, she became the capital of the United Soviet Socialist Republics.

Panorama of Komsomolsky Prospekt

Moscow Today

Although Moscow lost its official title as capital when Peter the Great founded his new city, for the common people Moscow was still the heart of their country and daily life went as before. Even the Tsars returned to the Kremlin to be crowned and its bureaucratic machinery creaked on.

In fact, although critical social unrest had struck Petrograd first, and the Revolution really started with the March on the **Winter Palace**, Moscow was so obvious the true capital that the first thing the Bolshiviks did, after consolidating their power was to declare Moscow the capital once again. From that moment the city never stopped growing, indeed its leaders once were determined to make it the political, if not the physical, capital of the world.

Lenin and Stalin

From November 1917 until he died in January 1924 Lenin devoted all his energies to providing government according to Marxist principles. Stalin then took power and in addition to carrying on the most rigid Party doctrine he injected his own special brand of dictatorial government which crushed all dissent. Moscow became a city of gigantism. Gigantic posters praising Communism, gigantic military parades, gigantic portraits of Stalin and Lenin, gigantic buildings of grandiose Stalinistic architecture.

But during Stalin's period Moscow started to grow beyond any conceivable limits of the past. The incredible subway system was finally started, enormous blocks of workers housing were erected and vast engineering projects of many kinds were undertaken. These were temporarily halted after the Nazi invasion on 22 June 1941 (Stalin had become the official head of government the month before) but they were again reinstated as part of a series of five-year plans soon after the joyous **victory parade** in Red Square on 24 June 1945.

Moscow became the greatest of the industrial and manufacturing centers attracting workers by the hundreds of thousands from all the republics. Unfortunately, government policies giving priority to the modernization of industry and to an unprecedent peacetime military capability, combined with an agricultural policy which forced individual farmers to become part of enormous state collective farms, soon caused great shortages in almost every sector of production. Moscow became known for its long lines at every store, for every item required for daily existence.

New district of Moscow

Red Square

Glasnost and Perestroika

When now president, **Michael Gorbachov**, became Communist Party Chief in 1985 he ushered in a new policy of Glasnost and Perestroika which has radically changed the lives not only of the Moscovites, but of all the Soviet Union and most of the Communist word. Now Moscow throngs with citizens from all fifteen republics, no longer restricted to their local areas, who bring with them their exotic customs and costumes.

Moscow is bright with flowers, many of them flown in to be sold in the markets and at the subway entrances. The subways are immaculate, the streets clean and crowds gather at corners to hear opinions which just three years ago would have meant imprisonment, the city has new life and every day more agreements are announced which will bring more consumer goods on the market.

For tourists Moscow is a city of excitement because they know its citizens are enjoying freedoms which they have not had for three generations. If life is still difficult, there is at least hope which the tourist shares. There is also an unending cavalcade of exhibits, sporting events, theatre, concerts and a multitude of other out-door events, which make Moscow the **City of Motion**.

Red Square and the Kremlin

(Metro Ploshchad Revolutsii)

Most visitors to Moscow first rush to the Red Square and the Kremlin. For group tours this is the first stop, and all guide books hurry their readers there as if it would all disappear tomorrow. In our humble opinion this is wrong, unless of course, one is spending only one day in the beautiful capital of **ancient Muskovy**. The Kremlin always beckons, the golden domes and crenelated towers are visible from almost anywhere in central Moscow and at night the five wind-blown ruby stars beam a glowing welcome. Savour the romance and mystery a little longer. First get a feel of the city and its people before beginning your tourist rounds. Start with **Prospect Marx** or **Prospect Kalinin**, if you can. There are many beautiful and exciting things you will see and remember, but nothing will be as fascinating as this area, leave it for last, the highlight of your visit.

What is now known as Red Square had been a marketing area for many centuries. Around its center and along the Kremlin walls all kinds of products were available-anything that could be eaten or worn, bought or sold, even notched logs of many sizes with which to build the first prefabricated houses.

The square itself was a morass of mud, logs were constantly being thrown in walk upon and keep man and beast from disappearing forever. Around 1700, when Peter the Great had the square paved with cobblestones, it was called, Red Square, but the Russian word, 'Krasnaya', actually means 'grand ' or 'beautiful', the connotation of red is a fairly recent one, popularized by the military marches and the massing of the red flags and banners of Communism.

Until 1930 entrance to the square had been through the **Voskresenskiye Gate**, built in 1680 with twin towers topped with the imperial eagles. This disappeared along with many other relics of the past in Stalin's 'modernization' programme. One has to admit that now there is a panascopic view of the area although at a sacrifice of historic intimacy.

As one enters the square the **State History Museum** is on the right, in the middle of the Kremlin wall in front of the **Senate Tower** the **Lenin Mausoleum** flanked by the famous marble reviewing stands, straight ahead the fairytale St. Basil's Cathedral with the **Monument to Minin and Pozharsky**, in front to the right. On the way back to the entrance on the left side is the infamous **Lobnoye Mesto**, or 400 year old execution platform (altough proclamations were also read out from here), and occupying most of the middle left is the famous **GUM Department Store**.

Throne of Ivan the Terrible

Sculpture of Lenin in Kremlin

Lenin Mausoleum

The simple but very impressive, Lenin Mausoleum is of marble and red granite with a mourning band of black iridescent labradore. A perpetual guard of honour, changed every hour on the hour, stands at the entrance as during opening hours an endless stream files by to view the body of Lenin encased in a glass casket.

Outside the mausoleum are graves of heros of the Communist party as well as famous war heroes and many international figures including the American, John Reed. One also sees many busts over the graves of the famous, among which is **Joseph Stalin** who at first was buried alongside Lenin. He was removed from the mausoleum by Krushchov, who by the way is burried at the **Novodevichiy Convent**. Behind, interred in the Kremlin wall itself are many others of fame, their urns marked by black stone nameplates.

Monument to Minin and Pozharsky _____

Beyond, one passes the **Saviour** (Spasskaya) **Gate Tower** through which official black limousines occasionally whiz by and then comes the fabulous St. Basil's, whose proper name is **Cathedral of the Intercession**. In front to the left is the monument to **Minin and Pozharsky**. It was erected in the middle of the square in 1818 and later moved to its present position during a time when extensive alterations were made in the square. It commemorates the two great heroes, one a prince, the other a butcher, who together ended a bitter period of Russian history when they drove the Poles out of Moscow and ended their occupation of Russia. The depth of the reverence felt towards these men by the Russian people can be judged by the fact that the monument was paid for by popular subscription, and it was the sculpted monument in Moscow.

St Basil's the Blessed _____

The Cathedral became known as St. Basil's the Blessed was enshrined here. Its real name stems from the fact that Ivan the terrible commissioned the church in 1555-60 to

Autumn in Kolomen skoe

celebrate his victory over the Tatars in Khazan which took place on the **Festival of the Intercession**. Part of the folklore concerning St. Basil's is the legend that after the church was completed Ivan had the architects, **Barma** and **Postick**, blinded so that they could never duplicate the Cathedral. If this is true recent research would indicate that only one architect was blinded. It seems that the nickname of Postnik Yakovlev was 'Barma' (the mumbler).

This building, above all others, seems to symbolize Russia for most foreigners. Certainly the fair-tale onion domes are unique in their brilliant colours and are a magnet to the eye. What is now an united whole was once a collection of nine chapels, each very highly decorated, which over the centuries lost their art and their lustre. A great deal of restoration work has taken place, however, but from the remaining untouched areas one can marvel at and appreciate the skill of those who so painstakingly make such brilliant restorations.

Each chapel has its own style of frescoes and painted flowers united by the ancient ikonosis in the maintower. Miraculously artists from the time of Ivan the Terrible live again. As you leave the church grounds brows over the museums booklets offered from a table in front of the entrance. You may see some not available elsewhere.

THE KREMLIN

Its Walls and Towers

(Metro Biblioteka imeni Lenina)

The Kremlin, a rough triangle of only sixty-eight acres, was once a wooded hill covered in pines bordered on one side by the **Moskva River** and on another by the **Neglinnaya River** now confined to a conduit and flowing under the **Alexandrovsky Gardens**. From the time immemorial it had been recognised as a natural site for fortification and as its importance grew the Kremlin was strengthened by ever-bigger walls and towers. In May, 1845 the cornerstone was laid for the **Tainitskaya** (Secret) **Tower** and the final walls and towers we see today (with countless repairs and coats of paint) were mostly completed ten years later.

Outside the walls there were moats, ditches and embankments with their attendant ramps and draw-bridges. The walls themselves, 3.5-6.5 metres high, were the state-of-the-art defenses of their time. A gallery ran around the entire top of the wall with firing platforms from

Moskva River

two to four metres wide and machiocolations (holes near the floor) and gulleys through which scalding water, tar and boiling oil gushed out over the heads of the besiegers.

The 2.235 length of the walls is broken at cannon-range intervals (so that the enemy could be fired upon from both sides) by twenty towers, three of them round, five with gates. The **Kutafya-Gate-Tower** was built outside the walls with a drawbridge and the **Trinity** stone **bridge** over the moat linking it to the Trinity Tower. The drawbridge is gone, but this is still the main entrance to the Kremlin.

The tower bases were filled with food or ammunition supplies, some had wells and others secret passages (the Tainitskaya had a secret passage leading to the Moskva-hence its name). The last tower to be built, and the highest at 80m, is the **Trinity** (troitskaya) **Gate Tower**. The main tower is the **Saviour (Spasskaya) Gate Tower**, and looking closely one can see where its ikon has been chipped away. This tower contain the famous Kremlin clock and chimes. The clock mechanism takes up three tiers and the three weights are enormous, the largest weighing in (!) at 224 kilos. It strikes every 15 minutes and the chimes peal out the International at six in the morning and at midnight.

The Famous Red Stars

After the Byzantine double-headed eagle was adopted by the Tsars this imperial emblem surmounted all the buildings of state, placed on each tower and spire of the empire. It would be interesting to know why this emblem of oppresion was not removed from the Kremlin towers until 1935 whereas all other symbols of autocratic authority had been erased in 1918.

In 1937 the Communist star was mounted on Trinity Tower, its hammer and sickle made visible at night by powerful searchlights. The emblem now also crowns the **Saviour, Nikolskaya, Borovitskaya** and **Vodorzvodnaya Towers**, however these stars have far more brilliance.

Each star differs in size (to harmonize with the shape and length of the tower it caps) with their points measuring 3-3.75 metres from the center and their weights are an incredible 1-1.5 tonnes. Their radiance is now active from within as lamps from 3.700 to 5.000 watts (cooled by ventilators) blaze through the triple-plated ruby glass set in stainless-steel frames. The stars can resist gale-force winds because they are mounted on ball-bearings, enabling them to turn in any direction. It requires twenty-seven kilos of gold to gild them.

Firestorms and Ashes

In the meantime the area within the walls had became crowded with churches and palaces and the mansions of rich boyors and merchant princes. Periodically the Kremlin was swept by firestorms which again and again destroyed these wooden buildings and their stone successors. Not even an imperial decree that all roofs should be covered with layers of sod could save them.

The flames were not always set by accidental sparks. Many times mongol hordes took the walls and left nothing but ashes in their wake. Insurrections, treachery and even revolts by the Kremlin Streltsky Guards also left the city with heaps of bodies and piles of rubble. It is a miracle that some fragments of the past still survive. It is well to remember this as we marvel at the splendour still remaining.

The City Within

As one passes through **Kutafya Tower** over the bridge and through the **Troitskaya Tower** it is ironic that the first building on the right is the newest and the most modern building in the Kremlin, the **Palace of Congresses**. One should first pause at the gate for a moment and reflect on part of its recent history. Here it was that a band of valiant Moscovites met the van-guard of Napoleon's troops on 2 September 1812 and tried to prevent them from capturing the Kremlin. Six weeks later the survivors were able to watch Napoleon's retreat from this gate. Their descendants cheered the entry of Lenin into the Kremlin on 12 March 1918. Shorts are not permitted, nor are large handbags. Smoking is also not allowed, and once within, guards keep crowds from crossing the white pedestrian lines marking how far one can approach the official government buildings.

Voskresenskiyi Gate

Palace of Congresses _____

This enormous building of marble glass and aluminum is far larger than it looks. To keep its modern appearance from overpowering the surrounding structures, the auditorium, which seats 6.000, was sunk 15 metres below ground. It was constructed in the amazing time of one year in 1961 when **Nikita Khrushchov** (1953-64) had it built as a rival to the UN building. Its banquet hall has a capacity for 2.500 people. It does serve a useful purpose because in addition to the many state functions which take place, there are also a wide variety of theatre productions staged here including performances of the Bolshoi. The building contains 800 rooms and they are well used for a multitude of services.

Council of Ministers Building _____

Further down and to the right of the Palace of Congresses beyond the **Obelisk of Commandmants of Kremlin** stands this monumental building constructed in 1776-1787 with a triangular shape, and wearing a green dome. Although this was a government building where state affairs were held, it was also the living quarters for Lenin, his wife, and his sister. Also on the second floor is his study with its revolving bookcases, designed by Lenin himself. This building embodies many architectural features and one is owed by its majesty.

Arsenal _____

The original Arsenal was constructed according to the plans of Peter the Great between 1702-1736 but its present appearance is a result of changes when it was rebuilt after being partially destroyed upon Napoleon's retreat from Moscow. Originally designed to store arms, ammunition and the trophies of war, the Arsenal would still make Peter very happy. Lined across the front are 875 cannon, captured from Napoleon's frozen army, a highly visible monument from the former Senate building just across the square.

Cathedral Square _____

With the exception of the Armoury with its treasures, which we are saving for last, all the remaining important buildings are centered on this square which vibrates with history. Take a moment and try to imagine part of the pageantry which filled the air for five hundred years. How many thousands have been in the great processionals

St. Basil the Blessed

which celebrated Easter or crowned the Tsars, how loud did the bells ring in warning of danger, how dense the clouds of insence, how blinding the jewels of the church vestments and how magnificent the soaring chorales of the church liturgy!

Ivan I (Kalita), initiated construction in the square in the first quarter of the 14th century. During the previous centuries after the acceptance of Christianity by Vladimir, **Grand Prince of Kiev**, the Metropolitan, head of the Russian Church, had kept Kiev as the seat of ecclesiastical power. It was moved to Vladimir only when mortal danger from the Tatars hordes threatened. When Moscow became the capital of all the Russias politics and common sense dictated that it should also become the seat of Russia Orthodoxy. So it was that Ivan laid the cornerstone in what was to become Cathedral Square for the first stone church in Russia, the **Cathedral of the Dormition** consecrated 4 August 1427.

Cathedral of the Assumption

(Dormition of the Virgin)

This cathedral is the largest church and oldest structure in the square. It was meant to be, and remained the central church of the Russian state and when a new church of far greater splendour commissioned by **Ivan III** was completed in 1479 its solid foundations became the firm rock which bound church and state until **Peter the Great** tried to pry them apart again.

Here all the Tsars were crowned and here all the Princes of the Church received their authority. Some of the most venerable ikons of all Russia were brought to this cathedral as symbols of its importance. Restoration has revealed once again the richness of its decor and the magnificence of its altars. Among the national treasures stored here are the unique wooden throne carved in the shape of a tent from 1551 and used by **Ivan the Terrible**, the first to bring the title of Tsar to the throne. Another is the central chandelier, **the Harvest**, it is pure silver, forged from the plunder recovered as Napoleon's army fled Moscow and the fiery holocaust that nearly trapped Napoleon himself. If the domes of this cathedral do not seem to gleam quite as brightly as others in the square neglect is not the cause, but oxidation, their golden rays reflect the gleam of gilt, but the domes of the Cathedral of the Assumption reflects the gleam of sheets of pure gold.

Church of the Deposition of the Virgin's Robe

To the left of the *Cathedral of the Assumption* is the single-domed Church of the Deposition of the Virgin's Robe. The first church by the name was built in Constantinople in the fifth century to venerate a holy relic of the Virgin, a robe or a vail. It was believed that this relic miraculously saved, on several occasions, the city from its enemies. In 1451 a church by the same name was erected in Moscow to celebrate the repulse of an attack on Moscow by the **Crimean Khan Mazovshi**.

It was later destroyed in the great fire of 1473 but was rebuilt on the old foundation (1484-86) by the same architects and artisans who had worked on the *Cathedral of the Annunciation*. Originally it served as the private chapel of the Patriarchs, but when the Patriarchs Palace was built the chapel was linked to the Tsar's Palace and the *Cathedral of the Assumption* by covered wooden passages and became the private chapel for the Tsar and his family. In the centuries before Peter the Great the imperial family spent many hours each day in prayer.

Cathedral of the Annunciation _____

This church was built originally for **Grand Prince Ivan III** as his private chapel (1484-89) and restored in 1547 during the reign of Ivan the Terrible after another one of the fires which constantly swept Moscow. Its nine gilded domes cover some of the most treasured frescoes and ikons in all Moscow. In its original form it had only three domes, and the vaulted chambers of the basement contained the

Cathederal of the Assumption

treasure chest of princes and Tsars. At times foreign ambassadors were led down into the underground fortress to marvel at the wealth of the Russian court.

The Cathedral blazes with glorious art from the frescoes on the walls to the gold embossed doors and down to the polished agate-like jasper floor. The ikonostasis is from an earlier church, and the ikons, painted in 1405 by **Theophanes the Greek**, are magnificent examples of the Russian School of the 14th and 15th centuries.

The Archangel Cathedral

Facing the Cathedral of the Annunciation, this church with its five cupolas combines both Russian and Italian architectural elements, but one is immediately reminded of a Venetian palace. The ikonostasis is 13 metres high and of the many 15th-17th century ikons the one acclaimed to be the most outstanding is of its namesake, the **Archangel Michael**.

The Cathedral is most famous for the 54 graves and 46 sarcophagi containing the remains of so many of Russia's famous rulers which make it a sacred burial ground. Here are *Grand Prince Kalita, Prince Donskoy, Ivan the terrible* and *his sons*. Of special interest is the carved white-stone canopy over the tomb of Ivan's murdered son, *Dimitry*. (*Boris Godunov* is buried with his wife at *Zagorsk*). After 1712, when Peter the Great had built his capital in St. Petersburg, the Tsars were buried in the cathedral of the *Peter* and *Paul fortress*.

Mansion of the Merchant Dolgov

Patriarch's Palace and the Church of the Twelve Apostles

Together these two buildings serve as the **Museum of 17th Century Life and Applied Art**. The Palace was erected (1653-55) to serve as the residence of **Patriarch Nikon**, once almost more powerful than his Tsar, Alexi, father of Peter the great. The Church was added at the end of the 17th century. Displayed here is a fine collection of objects used in everyday life as well as a collection of rare books and manuscripts. Unique, and most interesting are the large stove used for preparation of the miro, or consetrated oil, and the enormous silver cauldron given by Catherine II in which the miro was kept.

Great Kremlin Palace

This palace, built between 1838-1849, was designed to be the official residence of the Tsars in Moscow. Although its facade, facing the Moskva, has three rows of windows, the building has only two floors. There are over 700 rooms in the palace which now also houses the **Supreme Soviet of the USSR**, the country's highest legislative body, and other chambers used for official business which are not open to the public.

The private apartments of the Tsar have been kept as they were and provide a fascinating glimpse into imperial life. The Palace also contains several halls named after the military orders of Russia. One of the most beautiful is that of **St George**, the patron saint of Moscow, where the highest orders and medals of the USSR are given out. The enormous chandaliers and the famous eighteen twisted columns are reflected in the polished parquet floor in which twenty different kinds of wood are fitted.

The Terem Palace

One is overawed by the magnificent palaces in Moscow but this one is the most memorable because of its charm and fairytale-like quality. It was built in 1635-36 as a very elaborate version of a typical Russian house. The name is derived from the Russian word for garret. The walls and ceilings are completely covered with beautiful flowers, intricately carved mouldings with stonework and window-architraves portraying fairy-tale animals.

Three windows still have the mica panes used before glass was common. Charming tile stoves and low ceilings give these apartments a very cosy atmosphere, the one exception to the normally grim appearance of Kremlin living quarters in that era.

Palace (or Hall) of Facets

This is the oldest surviving civic building in Moscow. Its name is derived from the stone facade carved like facets of a gem. Built in 1487-9, it has a similarly carved council chamber where the Tsars met with their appointed councilors and where foreign ambassadors were received. The hall, with an area of 495 square metres and nine metres high, is supported by a single pillar. Now used for staid state ceremonial occasions, its walls once rang from the toasts of **Ivan the Terrible** celebrating his victory over the Khazan Tatars and **Peter the Great** drinking his couriers under the carved wooden table in triumph over his arch-enemy, Charles XII of Sweden.

Tsar Bell Tower

Often called, '**Ivan the Great Bell Tower**', it actually was finished in 1600, during the reign of **Boris Godunov**. Eighty-one metres high, it is the tallest structure in the Kremlin, and until the first highrise built after the Second World War, it was also the highest structure in Moscow. The Tower is gilt-domed, white, octogonal shaped and of brick. Twenty-one highly ornamented bells, including the **Assumption Bell** weighing 70 tons, hang in the belfry.

Tsar Bell

The Tower is actually a complex of building which consist of the tower, the belfrey and the **Filaret Building**. On display are very old ornate Russian Orthodox vestments.

Tsar Bell

Standing near the Bell Tower is the Tsar Bell, at 210 tonnes the largest bell in the world. It is 6.14m high with a base diameter of 6.60m. It was cast in 1735-36 of nearly 80 per cent copper and highly decorated with relief portraits, ikons and inscriptions. Its appearance is somewhat flawed by the absence of a 11.5 ton chunk which is placed beside it.

Guides tell you this fragment occured when the bell cracked while being sprayed with water. On 29 May 1737 there was another of the catastrophic fires which raged through the area and fearing the bell would melt under the intense heat it was cooled with water. An eyewitness reported, however, that the flames, having devored all the surrounding wooden buildings, reached the tower and caused several of the bells to fall. He went on *'a burning beam broke the rim of the Qween of Bell's in the fall..'* The bell had been cast successfully in November of the previous year but it had been impossible to hoist the monster bell from the casting pit. This was not accomplished until one century later.

Tsar Cannon

This is mounted not far from the Bell. The **Moscow Cannon-Yard** was set up at the end of the 15th century and in 1586 this 40 ton bronze behemoth was cast to help defend the Savior Gate of the Kremlin. Fortunately, it was never needed, and, with its 890mm calibre and length of 5.34 metres, it remains the largest cannon in the world.

The iron cannon balls one sees are purely decorative. It is believed that crashed stone would have been used. (During time of siege it was common for hollow shot filled with messages to be fired over the rampart walls to relief forces camped beyond the perimeters of the besiegers). The cannon rests on a highly ornamental carriage added in 1835.

The Armoury and the Diamond Fund

This building stands next to the **Grand Kremlin Palace** near the **Borovitskaya Tower** and it contains the most popular exhibits in the Kremlin. Perhaps this is because not only are most of the items on display of unparalleled value and interest, but because after the immensity of the palaces and cathedrals, it is comforting to be overwhelmed by objects nearer one's own size.

The present building was constructed in 1851 as an art museum, however it is built over the site of the Kremlin's 16th century armoury which both manufactured and stored weapons and armour. This most fascinating (and expensive) exhibition both the relics of the past and the wealth of an empire. The oldest exhibit is the coronation cap of **Prince Vladimir Monomakh**, used to crown all the Tsar's up to Peter the Great.

The vast array of items includes the sabres of **Minim** and **Pozharsky**, a silver embroidered gown of Catherine the Great (one of the 15.000 she owned after a palace fire had completely destroyed her first wardrobe), precious art objects, many of them gifts of state to replace those lost in the fire, the best collection of old English silver in the world (Cromwell, melted down countless irrepracable specimens), and an endless list of other treasures.

Here you can also see a fabulous collection of Tsar's thrones, including those of Ivan the Terrible, Boris Godunov and the double-throne of Tsars Ivan and half brother Peter (they were crowned in such a hurry that their first throne was an ordinary one simply divided down the middle).

Nowhere is there a more valuable assembly of coaches, royal carriages (one presented by Qween Elizabeth I), and carriage sleds. These were really carriages on runners rather than wheels. Many were very richly furnished with shelves and books small windows and sables for beds. Hot stones or cannisters of pewter filled with hot water were used to keep out the freezing temperatures, these were not entirely successful because there were frequent complaints that at thirty degrees below zero even the fine wines and brandies froze!

Tourists are always fascinated by the Diamond Fund which is a collection of some of the most fabulous jewels in the world. When it was started by **Peter the Great** they could all be stores in one chest. **Catherine the Great** had a collection of 10.000 gems which took two strong men to carry, the caskets transported in long baskets! One of the prized jewels is the **Orlov Diamond**, a stone of 199 carats tinged bluish-green. It came from a mine in India, was cut in Amsterdam and given to Catherine by her lover. One of the fabulous gems of the world, Catherine did not keep it for herself, but had it mounted in the royal sceptre.

The Diamond Fund also contains the **Faberge eggs** Lenin did not sell, the largest emerald in the world, the largest gold nugget, the **Big Triangle**, weighing 3.6kg, another diamond, of 89 carats, given by the Shah of Persia to Nicholas I as compensation for the murder of a Russian ambassador when a mob stormed the embassy. Considering that what one see in these exhibits and the entire Kremlin, a trip to Moscow is truly a trip of a lifetime.

Faberge Egg

> **INFOTIP:** Children under the age of 16 are not admitted to the Diamond Fund. The largest collection of Faberge ever exhibited are now on tour, including many from the collection publisher Malcolm Forbes, who owns more Faberge eggs than the Kremlin.

THE MUSEUMS OF MOSCOW

There are so many museums in Moscow that the only way one could see them all is to actually live there, and new ones are opening all the time. Most not only have incredible exhibits, they have fascinating histories as well. Although many of them are housed in buildings created to be used as museums, a great number of the museums formerly were palaces of the nobility or mansions of incredibly rich merchants.

Tsars rewarded the nobility and the **boyers** (originally advisors to the Grand Princes) for their advice and loyalty with large estates together with thousands of serfs to work them. This was especially true when nobles were sent to open vast new tracts of land acquired by the State. Without the forced repatriation of this enormous pool of serf labour the vast hinterlands would also remain a potential threat to the central power of Moscow. The merchants, many of them foreigners, grew rich beyond imagination when they were able to harness the benefits of the Industrial Revolution to this enormous backward country.

With this wealth and serf labour palaces and mansions were built to equal, and even surpass any of those in the West. To fill them the England and the Continent were scoured, the finest European artisans imported, collections were bought en masse, from chandeliers to carpets, cutlery to coaches and the walls were hung with paintings from all the masters.

In the meantime the serfs, by the hundreds of thousands were turning out masterpieces of their own. From architects to armourers native craftsmen created palaces, mansions and monasteries together with much of their contents. All this creativity was stimulated by Russia's rulers determined to erase forever the uncouth image of Russia which had prompted the scathing remark that Russians were no more than '*baptized bears*'.

All private property (except that of the Church) was confiscated in a sweeping proclamation by Lenin on 3 July 1918 who declared that it 'belonged to all the people'. With a stroke of the pen incalculable treasures were frozen in place, including those of the Tsars and their palaces.

Statue of Pushkin

INFOTIP: In the Soviet Union a Museum can be a cathedral, a palace, a monastery or an entire architectural complex. Their opening and closing times and days not only vary considerably, they also change from summer to winter. You can easily check with your hotel Intourist desk service. The best plan is to determine the sites you wish you wish to see and then choose your itinerary around their hours of operation.

Pushkin Fine Arts Museum

12 Ulitsa Volkhonka-Metro Kropatkinskaya

This is the one museum you must visit if you have an interest in art. Only the Hermitage in Leningrand has a larger collection of foreign art. Its French School of paintings from Neo-Classical to the modern has given it an international reputation. It opened in 1912 as a museum for classical sculpture with casts made from the works of antiquity and the Rennaisnance. The idea was for Russian students to be able to study the finest works of the past without having to go abroad. There are now also many Greek originals.

When the State expropriated private collections many of them were brought here as well as other works of art from Leningrand museums. A visit of several hours would be required to do this museum justice. In the basement there is a small book stand and a wardrobe for coats and parcels.

Facade of Tretiakov Gallery

Tretyakov Art Gallery

Lavrushinsky Pereulok 10-Metro Novokuzetskaya

This is monumental exhibition of Russian national art. The collection of over fifty thousand paintings and ikons are an historic survey of art in Russia from the 11th century to the present. Founded by **Pavel Trelyakov** (1832-98) who, with his brother **Sergey**, started the collection in 1856. It was presented to the City of Moscow in 1892 and taken over by the State with the expropiation proclamation of 1918. Other collections were added and new buildings were erected to house them.

Museum of Folk Art

Stanislavskogo Ulitsa 7-Metro revolyutsii Ploshad

Contains peasant folk art beginning from the 17th century. Handicraft wares and household items such as, paintings, wood carvings, lace and much more from the finest craftsmen of Russia during the centuries.

The Andrei Rublev Museum of Early Russian Art

Ploshad Pryamikova 10-Metro Taganskaya
Formerly the **Andronikov Monastery**, this museum features rare ikons and paintings by Russian masters from the 15th-17th centuries. During the summer there is a special organized tour by Intourist.

From Ostankino Palace Museum

Ostankino Palace of Serf Art

Pervaya Ostankinkaya Ulitsa 5-Metro VDNKH
This 18th century palace houses a fabulous collection of works from 18th century West European masters. Its unique feature, however, is the remarkable collection of **Russian serf art**. There is also a palace theatre where elaborate productions were staged with scenery and performances done entirely by the estate serfs.

Kuskovo 18th Century Estate-Museum and Museum of Ceramics

Ulitsa Yunosti 2-Metro Ryazansky Prospekt

A magnificent estate with a lake and a large park dotted with statues and guesthouses. It features a priceless collection of ceramics and porcelain brought here from other museums. Among the pieces are several which won prizes for designs in Socialist themes.

Peter the Great gave Kuskovo to Count **Petr Borisvich Sheremetiev** as a reward for helping defeat his long-time enemy, Charles XII of Sweden at Poltava. When the Count married Varvara Cherkassakava in 1743 she brought, among other things, as part of her dowry the estate of Ostankina and 60.000 serfs. Together they owned roughly three million acres of land, including 1.200 villages and 200.000 serfs. They often entertained at Kuskovo 1.500 guests at a time.

Moscows Animal Theatre

Bakhrushin Central Theatre Museum _____

Ulitsa Bakhrushina 31/12-Metro Paveletskaya
If the theatre has any fascination for you at all, this is the museum you simple can't miss. It has a magnificent collection of personal items belonging to famous artists and many of the props they used as well as 200.000 photographs of the artists and of productions in which they appeared. Here is a sweeping survey of the theatre covering two centuries.

Glinka Museum of Musical Culture _____

Ulitsa Fadeyeva 4-Metro Nayakoskaya
This museum has an extraordinary collection of musical instruments and music scores, many with the original annotations of the composer. It is also the center of a modern mystery and fight between the State and the grandson of the world-famous basso, **Chaliapin**. The grandson is claiming that a recently discovered home-movie made by Chaliapin was stolen from his house and is stored here. He wants it back but the State denies that it has this twenty-minute amateur production.

Ostankino Palace Museum

Blue Hall of Ostankino Palace Museum

Kolomenskoye Museum Preserve _____

Proletarsky Prospect 31-Metro Kolomenskaya

For centuries there had been a small village on the banks of the Moskva River just outside Moscow called Kolomenskoye. During the 14th century this beautiful location became popular as a summer retreat for members of the highest nobility. In 1671 **Alexi Romanov**, father of Peter the Great, began to build his own timber palace which came to be known as the Eighth Wonder of the world.

It consisted of an icredible array of 24 buildings with connecting latticed stairways, balconies, porches, arcades and courtyards which had an exotic collection of tent roofs, onion domes and pyramidal towers which capped this fantastic hodge-podge of timber and shingle. There were three thousand windows of mica (used before glass became common), some of them coloured and framed in tin to look like stained glass windows. There were baths for the royal family, their guests and even the servants.

ARCHITECTURAL MUSEUMS

The Bears of the North and the Sun of the West

In the same period the 'Sun-King', Louis XIV of France was building his palace at Versailles which became a world-wide symbol of luxury and ostentation. Within these rooms of gold, marble and silk there was not a single bath, not a toilet. At the same time that Russian envoys to his court were being called 'Baptized Bears', King Louis refused to eat with a fork saying that he had eaten with his fingers all his life.

The palace was used by Peter the Great but after he moved the capital to St Petersburg it was increasingly negleted and finally abandoned. Catherine II had the structures surveyed and decided the cost of repairs would be too great and had the complex demolished. Before doing so however, she had an exact replica made, one-fortieth of the original size. Both Catherine and Alexander I had wooden palaces built here but these were also torn down, in the 20th century.

Masterpieces of Russian Rennaisance

In the 16th, 17th and 18th centuries there was a great building rennaisance in Russia and what one now sees on the estate is not only buildings erected through the centuries on these grounds but many more moved here from other locations. The royal residences were designed to be approached from the river but the present entrance is the Spassky (Back) Gate which once was the service entrance. Immediately one sees through the trees the blue onion domes of the Church of the Kazan Okon of the Mother of God.

A splendid example of a Front Gate is located in the east section of the estate. It has four tiers and two passageways, the larger for coaches, the smaller for pedestrians. The most striking and the most important of the buildings erected here is the tent-roofed Church of the Ascension.

One of the most interesting of the buildings moved here is the four-room hut used by Peter the Great in Arkhangelsk. It is furnished with household items commonly used at the end of the seventeenth century. It also contains Peter's bed which not only looks very uncomfortable (which would be in keeping with the ascetic life he led) but also far too short for his six foot seven inch frame until one remembers that it was the fashion at the time not to sleep stretched out, but to lie propped up on enormous pillows.

Often there are young artists with their wares outside the entrance. Their work is exceptionally good and, with a little bargaining, well worth what they are asking for beautifully and intricately hand-painted broaches and wooden eggs.

Ancient Crown of Russian Tsars

From the Grand Kremlin Palace

Museum of the 17th Century Architecture and Painting

(*Church of the Holy Trinity in Nikiniki*) *Nikitnikov Pereulok 3*

Described as the **'jewel of merchant architecture'**, it is ironic that this beautiful little church built in 1634 by one of Moscow's great capitalists is hidden behind the Central Communist Party Committe Headquarters. Grigory Nikinikov, merchant prince and finacier, had the church built in gratitude for the many favours ha had received from the government in return for his help in financial affairs.

This museum is worth seeing because of its 'fairytale' appearance, but its real interest lies in the wall paintings which depict the daily life of seventeenth century Russia. The robust scenes remind one of Brueghal and they are quite a change from the stylized formality of religious art. Often very beautiful posters are sold here.

Danilovsky (ST.Daniel) Monastery

(*Residence of the Patriarch of Moscow and all Russia*) *Danilovsky Vall Ulitsa 22-Metro Tulskaya*

In 1282 Prince Daniel, later **St Daniel**, who had inherited the Principality of Moscow as his share of his father's estate (which happened to be much smaller than the estates inherited by his two elder brothers) founded the first monastery in Moscow. He built a wooden church named after his patron saint, St Daniel of the Pillar, and

later built two others in Moscow, the **Monastery of the Epiphany** in 1296 and in 1300 the other in Krutitsy.

Like all monasteries at the time, St Daniel's also served as a fortress and saw the invansion of a Tatar army (brought in by one of his brothers) and the attack on Moscow in 1301 by **Prince Konstantin of Ryazanin**. With the death of Prince Daniel in 1303 the Monastery began a long decline but was saved by a series of miraculous healings which took place at his grave within the Monastery.

In 1547 Ivan the terrible had it reorganized and built a new church. In 1591 its ramparts helped fen off an attack on Moscow by the **Crimean Khan Kaza Girei** and in 1606, when Moscow was again beseiged, this time by the peasant armies of **Ivan Boltnikov**, it sheltered the troops of **Tsar Vasily Shirisky**. The False Dimitry II burned it to the ground as he fled Moscow, but is was rebuilt and in 1652 (716 by the old calendar) Prince Daniel was canonized.

During the retreat of Napoleon in 1812 the silver framework from St Daniel's tomb was stolen. This was, however, the nadir of the Monastery's fortunes. By the 1920's it had gained a high repute as a theological school and in 1983 full restoration of the cloister began. In now performs all the functions of an active monastery as well as being the **Residence of the Patriarch**. It is also a center for scholars because it not only has many religious works in the original, but also has a large collection of manuscripts in microfisch, including many from Constantinople.

Donskoy Monastery

Donskaya Ploshad 1-Metro Shabolovskaya

Like the other monasteries, the Donoskoy was built not only as a religious retreat but as a fortress to withstand attacks on Moscow by the everinvanding hordes of Tatars. The Donoskoy, however was constructed by **Tsar Fedor** in 1591 as a thank-offering after the Crimean Tatars of Khan Kaza Gieri had already retreated.

It was named after the miracle-working Ikon of the **Donskaya Virgin** which had been carried into battle by **Prince Donskoy** who routed the Tatars on the banks of the **Don** in 1380. Believing the Ikon could again save them the Tsar had it brought to the expected site of battle. During the night the Ikon appeared to the sleeping Khan as a celestial vengeance showering his troops with arrows. In the morning he retreated without a battle and Moscow was saved once again.

Although this monastery is not as beautiful as the incomparable **Novdechiy Convent**, nor as large as **Danilov Monastery**, it is slowly being restored and its grounds contain many historical treasures. Some of the earlier tombstones still show traces of colour from when it was fashionable to paint them. The brick walls and towers were

Typical 17th Century Church Tower

Star crossed steeples

built in 1711. When Stalin was rampaging through Moscow destroying irreplacable treasures from the past to construct Socialist monstrosities, the **Holy Saviour Church** was razed and some of the remnants were brought here. Embodded in the walls are fragments which include bas-reliefs of Deborah, St Sergius blessing Dimitry Donskoy before the Battle of Kulikovo.

In 1934 Stalin also removed the **Arch of Triumph** commemorating the victory over Napoleon and had its parts stored here. When, after the Second World War, it was again erected some parts were left in the Monastery garden. The Monastery also houses the models of over 150 sculptures which have been made as protypes for one to be chosen as a monument to Stalin's victims.

The Monastery was the scene of a bizarre incident in 1771 when Moscow was swept by a form of the plague which seemed to be killing more women than men. They came by the multitudes to kiss a 'healing' ikon of the Blessed Virgin. To stop the spread of infection Archbishop Abrose removed the ikon. Not understanding his motives, a hysterical mob attact the monastery and killed the Archbishop. His remains lie in the curved metal vault to the left of the ikonostasis in the 'old' Cathedral of the Donskaya Virgin.

Novodevichiy Convent Museum _____

Novodevichiy Proyezd-Metro Sportivnaya

The golden domes and red towers of this magnificent ensemble of Moscow Baroque buildings are visible from the tree tops as one cruises down the **Moskva River**. The sight is unforgettable and the awe it inspires is only magnified when standing outside the walls.

Prince Vasily III started construction of this Convent in 1524 to celebrate the capture of **Smolensk** from **Lithuania** who had controlled this strategic city of the Kievan princes for over one hundred years. The beautiful **Cathedral of Smolesk** was built first and gradually other churches and the surrounding walls were added. Although it was built as a fortress supplementing others that guarded the approaches to Moscow, its primary function was to provide a retreat for ladies of the royal court who not always took the veil voluntarily.

'Get thee to a Nunnery' _____

Many were victims of court politics and when the influence of their families waned there was no other place for them since they were not allowed to marry beneath their station. It was also a convenient place to get rid of troublesome or over-ambitious women such as Peter the Great's half-sister, the Regent Sophia, who was not satisfied with power behind the throne, but wished to occupy the throne complete with rob and sceptre.

These banished ladies had great fortunes at their disposal which they lavished on the Convent. One can only imagine the inward despair which turned to pity and embellished the walls with some of the finest fescoes in the world.

After the death of Sophia the Convent was turned into an orphanage and suffered neglect until the **Romanov Empress** once again supported the Convent and it was gradually to its former glory. Napoleon ordered the Convent burned to the ground (Since it is claimed that so many of Moscow's architectural treasures were destroyed by Napoleon one begins to wonder about the truth of these statements) but miraculously a nun knew how to defuse the explosives and the convent was saved. In 1922 the Convent was converted into a **State Museum** and it has been completely restored.

For the past year the new cemetary has been opened to the public but the hours are highly erratic. It closes without warning, the reason often given that a funeral is in progress. The cemetary is worth trying to see because of the many unusual monuments it holds, including those of

Soviet leaders politics have kept them from being buried in the Kremlin. One of the largest and best *Beriozka shops* is across from the Convent.

Foreign Affairs building

Museum of the History and Reconstruction of Moscow _____

Novaya Ploshad 12-Metro Dzerzhinskaya

Once the **Church of Saint John the Divine**, this classical building holds exhibits of Moscow's architectural past and models for the future. It shows a fascinating insight to the growth and restructuring of one of the world's greatest cities.

MUSEUMS OF HISTORY & REVOLUTION

Historical Museum

Red Square 1-2-Metro Ploshad Revolutsii
This museum is one of the most important in the USSR because it has such a tremendous collection of material illustrating the history of Russia from prehistoric times to the present that it can not display even a fraction of it. Built in 1883, it was designed so that the facade would harmonize with other buildings in the Kremlin. As of this writing the museum was closed for repairs.

Central Lenin Museum

Ploshad Revolutsii 2-Metro of same name
The 34 halls of this museum contain thousands of papers and many of the personal belongings of Lenin (including the Rolls-Royces imported from England in 1919) reflecting not only his life's work but also the progress of the Communist Party. Among the manuscripts hand-written by Lenin are his decrees on Soviet power. This is probably the best museum in Moscow built for this purpose. The stately halls are hung with enormous canvasses depicting Lenin at work. Such paintings as

Lenin on the Speaker's Stand and Lenin at Smolny are 'absolutely true' in every detail, including a fly on the wall.

There is an exact replica of Lenin's office in the Kremlin as well as the overcoat he wore during an assassination attempt the bullet holes are in the cloth, crossed stiched in red. There are devices where one can hear a lecture on Lenin in Russian, English, French and German. It is also possible to see a half hour documentary. This is the only museum in Russia with escalators.

An interesting aspect of this museum is just how much longer, in view of the radical political changes taking place and the discreditment of Communism as a viable economic philosophy, it will remain as a monument to Leninism. Some have gone so far as to say that within ten years the Museum will be renamed and used for another purpose, and even that the Mausoleum will be converted, perhaps to a memorial for all Russians lost in war and called something like, '*Monument to Fallen Patriots*'.

Lenin Funeral Train

Metro (and railway station) Paveletsky

In 1923 Lenin spoke at a meeting of railway workers here who were repairing locomotive U-127. The workers elected Lenin an honourary locomotive engineer and when he died a year later this locomotive and coach No 1691 were sent to **Gorky** to return his body to Moscow.

The Former Shaliapin Museum

USSR Museum of the Revolution _____

Gorky Street 21-Metro Mayakovskaya

In another of history's ironies, this museum is housed in a beautiful old restored mansion with lions still guarding the gates of what once was the '**English Club**' of Russian aristocracy. Here are over one million exhibits including documents, paintings, sculptures etcetera, tracing the history of the Socialist Revolution in Russia from 1905-1917. The library has a foreign section containing literature in 34 languages, concerning the revolutionary movement.

In front of the museum stands the gun fired by the revolutionary soldiers when they shelled the White Guards in October, 1917. When the guns of the cruiser **Aurora** fired signalling the storming of the Winter Palace in Petrograd (formerly St. Petersburg, now Leningrad) it was a shot literally heard around the world. A section of the armour plating from this ship is exhibited here. Admision free.

Museum of Carl Marx & Friedrich Engels _____

Marska i Engelsa Street 5-Metro Kropotkinskaya

This museum contains a complete history of the lives and works of these men including original manuscripts, first editions of their works and a photographic survey of them and their associates.

Moscow 1820

Kalinin Museum

Marx Prospect-Metro Kalininskaya

A peasant's son, a national hero and President of the Supreme Soviet from 1919 until 1946, this comrade of Lenin is memorialized in a small elegant mansion with a fine collection depicting his life and works.

Christ Saviour Cathedral

Central Museum of the USSR Armed Forces

Sovetskoi Armii Street 2-Metro Mira Prospekt

As you might guess, this museum is devoted entirely to the achievements of the Soviet armed forces detailing their history and activities with Warsaw Pact countries. Of special interest to visitors from the USA is the U-2 reconnaissance plane shot down over Siberia with pilot Gary Powers in 1960.

Panorama Museum of the Borodino Battle _____

Kutuzovsky Prospekt 38-Metro Kutuzovskaya

This building is easy to recognize, from the outside it looks like a turquoise drum. Although inconclusive as a battle, the **Battle of Borodino** was an important one in Russian history. On 26 August 1812, near the village of Borodino, Napoleon's Army of 135.000 men with 587 guns battled the Tsar's troops of 120.000 men and 640 heavy guns commanded by **General Kutuzov**. This titanic struggle lasted 15 hours and ended with Napoleon's first defeat, altough he was able to recover enough to go on and capture Moscow, only to abandon it six weeks later amid great misery on both sides. In September of 1876 **Lev Tolstoy** visited Borodino and reconstructed the plan of battle he later described so unforgettably in his monumental **War and Peace**.

The Museum contains many souvenirs of the battle including some of the weapons, standards and other artifacts of the battlefield. One is surprised at the sizes of the uniforms which show the small stature of the combatants. There are several large paintings including the famous scene when General Kutuzov made the soul-tearing decision to abandon Moscow.

From the History Museum Moscow

The Baton of a Field Marshal

Only the Cannon's Roar and the Acrid Smell of Gunsmoke are Missing _____

The actual **Panorama** was originally created by F.A. Rouband in 1912 but later years saw great deterioration and neglect, but, it was restored in the 1950's and housed in a more suitable building than the present one, where it was moved and re-exhibit in 1962, the 150th anniversary of the battle. The Panorama is a complete circle 115m long and 14m high, the second largest painting in the world.

It is beautifully painted and brilliantly stateged a true attraction even if one is not normally interested in war scenes. The viewing platform is 13 metres from the wall, the distance between realistically constructed as part of the battlefield. Burned out huts abandoned campfires (with embers still glowing), ruined cannon and the general debris of war are vividly recreated. The painting is almost memorizing, needing only to smell of gunsmoke and the sounds of battle to make it terrifying. Even the pitiful slaughter of the horses is depicted. The overwhelming authenticity of the Panorama was made possible because every detail was copied from a photograph taken at the height of battle at midday on August 26 (September 7) 1812.

Standing before the entrance to the **Borodino Panorama** is an equestrian **statue of Kutuzov** and in a park nearby is a replica of the hut (the original burned down) where in the village of Fili on the outskirts of Moscow, Kutuzov held a council of war to determine the feasibility of defending Moscow. Tolstoy vividly portrays the scene in War and Peace and repeated the worlds of Fieldmarshal Kutuzov which are now inscribed on the granite obelisk standing near the hut: '*The loss of Moscow does not mean that the whole of Russia is lost. I order you to retreat for the sake of your Motherland*'.

The **Arch of Triumph** celebrating the defeat of Napoleon is once again a landmark, standing further down Kutuzovsky Avenue in **Victory Square**. The Arch was first constructed in 1827-34 and placed in the middle of the main road leading from St. Petersburg to Moscow where the Tsar and his Court passed through it on official visits. In 1934 Stalin had the Arch removed as part of his 'modernization' of Moscow and its components were stored at the Donskoy Monastery. After the Second World War the Arch was rebuilt on this spot although one can still see some of the original parts in the Monastery.

Literary Museums

No other country has idolized its artists and writers more than Russia. As you discover, parks and plazas, streets and museums are named after them and Moscow is filled with their statues or at the very least a plaque to show where they lived or worked.

The State Literary Museum

Trubnikovsky Pereulok (near Petrovka Street)

As with the **History Museum**, only a fraction of its collection can be displayed at one time, even with its many branches for individual authors. Among the priceless works, photographs, etcetera are many voice recordings, actual recitals by many of the most famous authors such as Tolstoy, Gorky, Pesternak and Evgeny Evtushenko.

The museum's branch feature works of M. Lermontov, A. Herzen, A. Chekhov, F. Dostoyevsky, and many others. All these museums are forever being closed for repairs and reopened again when completed. With Moscow so rich in museums the repairs and renovations required to keep these buildings, most of them over a century old, in operation is staggering. The two most popular literary museums, **Tolstoy** and **Pushkin** are within one block of each other, they are also closed. We were able to visit the Pushkin Museum, however, and since it is representative

State Childrens Music Theatre

of all the others and because Pushkin remains, to the Russian public, the most beloved of all, we will take you through the Museum hoping that soon it will once again be open to the public.

Pushkin Museum

Kropotkinskaya U1. 12/2-Metro Kropotkinskaya

The rambling mansion which houses this museum was built in 1814 by the famous architect, **A.G. Grigoriyev**, whose many Empire-style buildings are still scattered throughout Moscow. Although there is no historical connection with Pushkin the museum gives one the impression that he could have lived here. It was constructed of wood but, as was popular in that period, covered with stucco made to look like stone. When reopened it will have over ten halls featuring thousands of exhibits, many of which were given by an adoring public.

There are hundrends of Pushkin's works in many languages and editions (some entire collections confiscated by Lenin) and mementeos from theatrical productions of his works. There are many paintings of Pushkin, his wife and intimate friends as well as a remarkable bust quite unlike the usual static head and shoulders variety.

Pushkin's maternal grandfather, **Ibrahim Hannibal**, was an Abyssinian prince bought as a slave by the sultan in Constantinople and sent as a present to Peter the Great. The Tsar gave the slave his freedom and sent him to study in Paris. Later, in keeping with his beleif that promotion should be based on meritocracy rather than primogeniture, Peter sent him as an officer to the army where he was eventually promoted to General of the Artillery.

As a giant in Russian literature Pushkin was a great inspiration to aspiring writers. One of these, **Nadezhda Durova**, was also part of the curious phenomena which appeared throughout the Napoleonic Wars-after the battles, many women were found on the battlefield wearing soldier's uniforms. Durova was luckier than these and after surviving both the combat and retreat during Napoleon's invasion of 1812, she was encouraged by Pushkin to write her memoirs, **'The Cavalry Maiden'**.

One of the halls is devoted to the **'Duel and Death of Pushkin'** who was killed in a duel over the honour of his wife. His death caused a great deal of turmoil not only because of his enormous popularity, but because it was also generally believed that his death was politically inspired.

> **INFOTIP:** With the exception of the Borodino Panorama Museum, Intourist has many brochures on all its museums in English. Kiosks and bookstores also sell a wide variety of material dealing with various museums. Intourist also conducts special tours of the literary museums.

Tours Around Moscow

As we indicated earlier, ideally Red Square and the Kremlin should be visited last, their unforgettable buildings and incredible treasures the capstone to your visit to the 'City of the Golden Domes'.

If possible, begin your visit to Moscow by spending a few hours strolling down a busy street where you can absorb a feel of the city and get an impression of life in the present before going on a journey to the past.

For this reason we have Started Tours with Gorky and Kalinin Avenues. Walk down these bustling thoroughfares, browse through the shops and stop to take note of some of the landmarks you might wish to visit later. In one hour's walk you will learn more than by reading newspapers for one year.

Golden domes

Gorky Prospekt _____

Metro Prospekt Marksa

Gorky Avenue begins at **Marx Prospect** with the painted red walls of the Kremlin in view (reached by using the underpass here) and ends at the **Byelorusskaya Railway Station** with **Pushkin Square** in the middle. This broad thoroughfare was once the narrow but prestigious **Tverskaya Street**, an exclusive residential area. When Stalin started his great face-lifting of Moscow, in the mid 1930's it was decided that what had once been an entree for triumphal marches of the Tsars would now become the avenue for showing off the might of Soviet power on its way to Red Square. With incredible feats of engineering entire buildings were moved back from 60-180 feet, sometimes even changing their axis of orientation.

At the Kremlin end Gorky Avenue is anchored by the **Fiftieth Anniversary of the October Revolution Square** appropriately renamed in 1967. In a steep upward climb you will pass the *Intourist Hotel* with its very large Beriozka store and at buildings Nos 9 & 11 pause for a moment to notice their facings of red granite blocks. The blocks were quarried in Finland and brought to Moscow by Hitler to be used in building a monument celebrating his victory over the Soviet Union.

At number 14 stands an early 19th century building with elegant appointments (seeming to distain the mundane activity it surrounds) oddly out of place for the many items of food sold here. Called **Food Store No.1**, it is one of the popular attractions of Moscow. Passing the **Dryzhba Bookshop** one comes to **Sovetskaya Square** which contains the building of the **Moscow City Council** across for which is the equestrian statue of **Prince Yuri the Long-Armed**, with a **statue of Lenin** behind.

Coming to **Pushkinskaya Square** we see the **Armenia**, a store selling specialties, including the famous wines, of Armenia. The statue of Prushkin was erected through public donations and dedicated on 6 June 1880. The foot of the statue is always covered with flowers. This is the Fleet Street of Moscow-Izvestia, the daring Moscow News and many others publish here. Soon Pushkin Square can boast the largest McDonald's in the largest world, selling their Big Macs for roubles.

At No 21, beside the **Stanislavsky Drama Theatre** is the **USSR Museum of the Revolution**. On the right-hand side of the street at No 25, is the exhibition hall for one-man shows of Soviet artists and a paradise for poster collectors because of its display of satirical posters. Heading towards Byelorussky Railway Station with its statue of **Maxim Gorky**, and where trains arrive daily carrying passangers

Gorky Avenue

from London, Paris, Vienna, Berlin, Warsaw, Oslo and Stockholm, you pass another square, **Mayakovsky**.

This great Soviet poet who glorified the Soviet Revolution had a tragic death, dying from a mysterious suicide. His presence is still felt from the statue dominating the square. Beyond this monument, at the west end of the square, is the famous **Peking Hotel** specializing in-quess what, while at the other end is the **Sofia Restaurant** whose dishes are gastronomic delights for gourments enjoying Bulgarian food.

The square of the Byelorusskaya Station once held the **Tver Gates**, originally a wooden arch, later the Arch of triumph, which moved to Victory Square and placed so that its facade topped by the pronze horse and Chariot of Victory faced **Poklonnaya Hill**. Here, on 2 October 1812, Napoleon awaited with his generals for the delegation from the Tsar to present him with the keys to the city. It never came.

Kalinin Prospekt

Metros Kalininskaya & Arbatskaya

This avenue, named after a Bolshevik hero and long-term head of the Communist state after he died in 1946, begins at the **Lenin Library** and ends at the **Moskva River** where on the far side one can see the famous **Ukranian Hotel**. Like Gorky Avenue, Kalinin Prospekt begins at the Kremlin walls.

The Kutafya Gate and Trinity Towers loom in the background while the colossus of the **Lenin Library** dominates the entire area of a block between Kalinin Avenue and Frunze Street. Its collection of 36 million items includes works in 91 of the languages spoken in the Soviet Union and 247 foreign languages as well. The new buildings, constructed over a period from 1928 to the fifties, were required when its acquisitions overrun the original library. The old Lenin Library began with the expropriation by Lenin of the Pashkov Mansion, built in 1786, and still considered to be one of the best classical buildings in Moscow.

It was once owned by a favourite General of Catherine the Great **Rumyantsev**, who won many battles against the Turks. When Nikolai Rumyantsev transferred his collection of rare books and manuscripts to Moscow from St Petersburg he retired and devoted the rest of his life to

Kalinin Prospekt

collection. The Lenin Library is responsible for storing a copy of every item printed in the USSR and keeps track of the 340 million examples of publications found in the other four thousand libraries of Moscow.

The first part of the avenue, as far as **Arbat Square**, goes through an area where palace employees of the Tsar lived and where later fine mansions were built and can be seen still at Nos 5 & 7. The chamber of the 17th century **Apothecary Department** have been restored at No 7 and here, too, is the **Shchusev Museum** of **Architecture**, its models photographs and plans a complete record of architecture in the USSR. Exhibitions of the architecture of other countries are held year-round. Further down, at the corner of Semashko Street, an armchair sculpture of **Kalinin**.

In some ways the most interesting building on the entire avenue is **Friend-ship House** at No 16. When the rich merchant, Arseny Morozov, visited Spain and Portugal in the 1890's he was charmed by the castles he had seen and upon his return he commissioned a mansion to be built according to his idea of a medieval castle.

The building with its fine portal, twin towers and beautiful grillwork, is studded with shells, the symbol of faith that medieval pilgrims always carried with them. When it was completed the mansion became famous all over Moscow as the '*Spanish residence*'. In 1959 it was opened as the **House of Friendship with Foreign Countries** and became a center for world-wide dissemination of Communist propaganda, with delegations arriving from all over the world. The top personnel are diplomats who have served in many foreign posts and who, if in the entertainment business, would be said to be 'between engagements'.

A little further down the avenue passes Arbat Square and on the right is the first giant 'skyscraper' in the Soviet Union, completed in 1924. Across from the Metro is a beautiful little church from the 17th century, **Church of Simon Stylites**, now the exhibiton hall for the **All-Russia Society for the Conservation of Nature**. Here one also sees the four new buildings housing government offices Moscovites call 'books', because each of the 26 storey buildings look like an open book.

Now come many stores and shopping areas including the **House of Book**, Moscow's largest book store (with a special department for stamp collectors), a supermarket, a beauty salon and many others which offer visitors a real cross-section of Moscow shopping. At the end of the avenue near the Moskva is a thirty-storey block of buildings which are the headquarters for Comecon, and just around the corner is the American Embassy.

Arbat Street

Metro Arbatskaya & Smolenskaya

This famed street, now a pestrian mall, is a center for all kinds of activity and artistic expression. Painters display and sell their works (some of it quite bad), musicians entertain , a Dixieland jazz band was popular enough to be shown on TV, and street orators practice their new found freedom. The only state owned video cassette store is here, 'filled with dull old socialist movies', (a quote from a bystander) and the street pulses with life all day.

Unfortunately some historic buildings have already been pulled down but there is a drive to preserve the one remaining in this ancient section of Moscow. From Arbat Square many lanes radiate through the area which was once the Saint Germain of Moscow and wandering through them one can see many old buildings and charming facades.

At Arbat Street No 42 there is the **Georgian Cultural Central** (Mziurey Little Sun) where, in addition to many displays of Georgian culture there are booths selling souvenirs from the Republic. Follow the black iron pole with its light brackets in the center of the room downstairs

A typical crowd on Arbat Street

and you will find a large typical Georgian tearoom. At 13 kopeks to a cup (16 with two sugar sticks), it is quite a bargain. Besides the special Georgian tea they serve 'Achma', a delicious noodle dish with bechamel sauce and cheese at only one rouble, 60 kopeks.

Although the walls have marble plaques and the columns are marble-sheathed, there are also lacquered blue panels painted with flowers which create an intimate atmosphere. This is a very good place for rest and refreshment.

Back on the street you might consider some of the large surrealistic canvasses (framed or unframed) or small wooden-framed moonlight land scapes. Painted wooden eggs, and the Matrushka dolls are also everywhere, but be sure to bargain. This is a tourist street, with the usual inflated prices.

At No 53 a memorial museum has been opened where Pushkin brought his bride for three months, and at the end of the square there is another memorial, a **statue of Gogol**. The most famous restaurant of the area is laso on the square, at the front, **The Praga**, one of the oldest and largest in Moscow, its specialty, the dishes of Czechoslovakia.

Lenin Hills

Metro Leninskiye Gory

This tour should be taken when the weather is good, you have two hours of free time and when you are surfeited with man's creative ingenuite and would like to breath in a little of nature's glory as well. Naturally **Intourist** has a tour, but you can take to the hills on your own. The Metro which takes you there and brings you back is different from all other stations in the system. Here the Metro crosses the Moskva River on a two-tiered reinforced concrete bridge 200 meters long.

The station is the glass-enclosed lower level where pedestrians can walk on either side while traffic whizzes by overhead. When getting out walk along in the same direction as the train and you will reach the right bank of the river. About 50 meters further along there is a glass-enclosed escalator which goes to the top of the hill. You will come out next to **Vorobyorskaya Highway** and to the right there is a peaceful shaded walk which leads to an observation platform a few minutes walk away. There all Moscow and the Moskva Riverlie spread before you. If you pause before going to the platform, you can see on the other side of the highway the **Moscow Palace of Young Pioneers**, an enormous complex devoted entirely to children, and typical of the care the USSR has lavished on its children. The buildings and grounds contain every possible kind of learning and recreational facility.

Beyond is the **New Moscow Circus**, a large circular building seating 3.500 spectators. The circus ring can be changed in a matter of minutes to accommodate an ice rink, an aquatic tank or become a stage for magicians.

Directly in front of the observation platform is the impressive Moscow **Lomonosov University**. The campus has an area of 790 acres include a sports stadium, a park and botanical gardens. The buildings consist of a 32 storey tower, the spire rising to 380 meters crowned by a golden star set in a wreath of wheat ears, and flanking wings with blocks of 12 and 18 stories. The towers of the taller buildings are set with clocks, their dials nearly nine meters in diameter.

This impressive edifice is, like the Taj Mahal, fronted by a reflecting pool and is one of the monumental structures designed when Stalin's dreams of building the colossal **Palace of the Soviets** in the Kremlin were drowned in the swampy sub-soil which once supported the **Holy Savior Church**. Eight buildings in all (another is the **Ministry of Foreign Affairs** directly across from the **Hotels Belgrade I & II**), representing the typical style of monstrous towering pomposity which all dictators seem to favour, were created from the materials gathered for the Palace.

When the University was completed (1949-53) it stood on the outskirts of Moscow. Now it seems to be at the city center. Surrounded by a sea of green-parks and gardens patched by lakes and ribbons of water, one stands in wonder and gazes out over the vast panorama of shapes, the ancient Kremlin domes, the blocks of modern buildings the **TV Tower** needle and the oval of Lenin **Central Stadium**.

Moscow from the Lenin Hills

USSR Economic Achievments Exhibition _____

Metro VDNKh (The Russian abbreviation of the name)

This is a lot more fun than it sounds, so if fun is your mood put on your best walking shoes and visit the exhibit halls of this huge park which has an ever-changing variety of 100.000 exhibits, more or less. It covers 533 acres, all of which can be reached at the end of **Mir Prospekt**. Pavillions from all the 15 republics, each built in its native architectural style, house displays of produce and hand-icrafts from these areas.

Each year there is an international book fair and throughout the year exhibitions from trade, industry and agriculture crowd the other 80 pavillions and hundreds of buildings in which temporary displays are arranged for thousands of visiting specialists.

A massive gate facade topped with enormous Socialist Art Statues of the Proletariat confront the visitor, but once past these there is a long promanade featuring fountains and art nouveau lamp standards shaped like ears of wheat which lead to the central pavillion, graced in front by a statue of Lenin.

The five halls of this building are a pictorial parade of propaganda for the glories of the Great October Socialist Revolution and they have gladdened the hearts of Communist visitors from all over the world as they wonder at such enormous paintings as, '*The Storming of the Winter Palace*' and '*Lenin Proclaims Soviet Power at the 2nd All Russian Congress of Soviets*'.

Dozens of vendors dot the grounds where one can buy snacks, souvenirs, stamps booklets about the exhibition, and of course, the ubiquitous and delicious ice cream. There is also a sight-seeing train which tours the grounds every 30 minutes, the fee is small and it saves time.

The most popular exhibition, for natives and visitors alike, is the **Cosmos Pavillion**. Its easily found because in front there is a launching platform with a rocket, which actually moves, duplicating the one used for the **Vostok spacecraft** of **Yuri Gagarin** which put him in space on 12 April 1961. As you approach, on the right side there is a row of chestnut trees, each planted by a Cosmonaut.

At this exhibition one sees the entire history of space, either with the actual space capsules, rockets and satellites or their models. Photographs, diagrams and samples of space rations, spacesuits and the full-size models of the **Soviet Soyuz** and the **American Apollo spacecraft** in July of 1975 nearly complete this exhausting display. The only thing missing is the model of the spacecraft in which poor **Laika** perished. This is sad because there once was, now she seems forgotten!

USSR Exhibition of Economic Achievements

Here is a good example of our suggestion to plan seeing together those sites close together. Outside this exhibition, to the left of the Metro, you will have seen the beautiful **Space Obelisk** soaring 96 metres in a silvery flight into space. The body of the obelisk is polished titanium (the largest object using this material) anchored to a granite base, rather ponderously designed in typical Socialist fashion in stark contrast to the ethernal structure poised above.

Adjoining the grounds are the **Main Botanical Gardens** and **Dzerzhinchy Park**. Here is the Ostankino Palace (see Architectural Museums) which can be seen along with the Exhibition and the Obelisk.

Alexandrovsky Gardens

Metro Ploshchad Revolutsii

This simple tour takes but a short time and is a welcome respite to the awe-inspiring complexities of the Kremlin. These gardens lie to the left of the Kutafya Tower (entry to the Kremlin) and contain the **Tomb of the Unknown Soldier**. Even since the gardens were laid out in 1820-21 their flower beds have provided brilliant displays of colour, delighting Tsars and Commisars alike. The entire garden lies on the bed of the **Neglinnaya River** which once joined the Moskva and now flows underground, led away by a large conduit.

In the middle of the garden along the central walkway which we will describe later, is an oddly-placed grotto, another memorial to be 1812 Patriotic War, and directly opposite stands a granite obelisk, a retreat, one might say. The shaft now has the names of many famous people who were deemed by Lenin to represent all those who either participated in or theorized on the Socialist Revolution. Dedicated in 1981, it was the first monument of the Revolution but before that it had been a monument to the **Romanov Dynasty** which the last Tsar dedicated in 1913 to celebrate 300 years of their rule.

Painting by Vasnetsov

Bolshoi Theatre

The main attraction of the gardens is the Tomb of the Unknown Soldier. The monument, one of the finest of its kind, lies at the foot of the Kremlin, secure in the wall. The grave is covered with bronze mantle, fringed and betasseled. In front there is a five-pointed bronze star embedded in a slab of black polished granite. In the center of the star burns an eternal flame which was lighted on 8 May 1967 by a torch brought from the **Field of Mars** in Leningrad where the fallen of the October Socialist Revolution are buried. The flame is reflected in a pool on which the star seems to float. It has become a tradition for newly-weds to come here and pay tribute directly from the wedding ceremony and to leave a bouquet of flowers. Unfortunately some misguided persons have recently begun to disturb the dignity and somber majesty of this memorial by throwing coins in the pool.

As part of the monument, parallel to the Kremlin wall, and marking the pathway which leads to the Grotto and the Obelisk there is a long line of red porphyry blocks. Buried under each is a container of soil from other cities which suffered the horrors of the Nazi invasion. The Unknown Soldier fell while defending Moscow in 1941. Inscribed on the tomb are the words,

'Your name is unknown. Your feat is immortal'.

OUT FOR A DAY OR TWO

Some excursions require a special permit (a fact Intourist does not always impart) and others might be closed, another secret held by that agency. Check with them before making plans.

The Arkhangelskoye Estate

28km.- 4hrs. This is a perfect example of something listed by Intourist, but impossible to see. It has been closed over four years with the prospect of rennovations going on for another ten. It is, however, one of the glories of Russia. Both the palace and the gardens are superb and the countryside along the way is beautiful. Its restaurant is famous and the magnificence of this complex makes it well worth the trouble when it is once again open. Official guides note that it is closed in damp weather and when the temperature reaches 20 below zero!

Palace of Archangelskoye Estate

State Circus on Vernodsky Prospekt

Lenin's House Gorky _____

35km.- 4hrs. This memorial is a mansion which Lenin periodically visited from the time he came to power in 1918 and where he lived from May 1923 until his death in January 1924. It contains all his personal effects and is preserved exactly as it was during his lifetime.

Abramtsevo Estate Museum _____

62km.- 7hrs. The mansion of this famous estate had, like many others of the time, a concert hall. Here many of the most brilliant figures of Russian art and literature came to visit and often to live. Three of those whose reputations were world-wide, to name but a few of the many, were Ivan Turgenov, Nikolai Gogol and Feodor Chaliapin.

115

Zagorsk History and Art Museum Preserve _____

71km.- 7hrs. Monastery of **Troitskaya Sergeeva**. Now named after the industrial complex spread outside its walls (in turn named after a Revolutionary hero), the actual title of this famous monastery is the **Laurel of St. Sergius under the Blessing of the Holy Trinity**. It was founded in 1340 by Sergius, a monk who himself built a small wooden cell and a chapel dedicated to the Holy Trinity. Sergius gradually became famous as was regarded as a Holy man because of his many good works. Prince Dimitry Donskoy came to ask his blessing before the Battle of Kulikovo against the **Tatar Khan Mamai**. When the Russians were victorious the monastery became a holy shrine and by the sixteenth century it had accumulated fabulous wealth donated by the nobles and Tsars who hoped to buy their way to salvation. Peter the Great took sanctuary here during his struggle with the Regent Sophia in 1689. The walls of the monastery, a mile in circumference, were twenty feet thick and once withstood a sixteen month seige by 30.000 Poles and Lithuanians.

Borodino Military History Field Museum _____

128km.- 8hrs. This the actual battlefield where Russians faced Napoleon in one of the most important battles of the Patriotic War of 1812. It contains many monuments and is constantly being developed as a tourist center.

Lev Tolstoy Estate-Museum
'Yasnaya Polana' _____

195km.- 13hrs. We probably know more about this estate where Tolstoy was born, lived and was buried than that of any other famous writer. Every aspect of his life is vivedly portrayed here.

> **INFOTIP:** Distances quoted in guides often vary. This happens because some measure from the center of Moscow, others from the outskirts.

State Children's Music Theatre

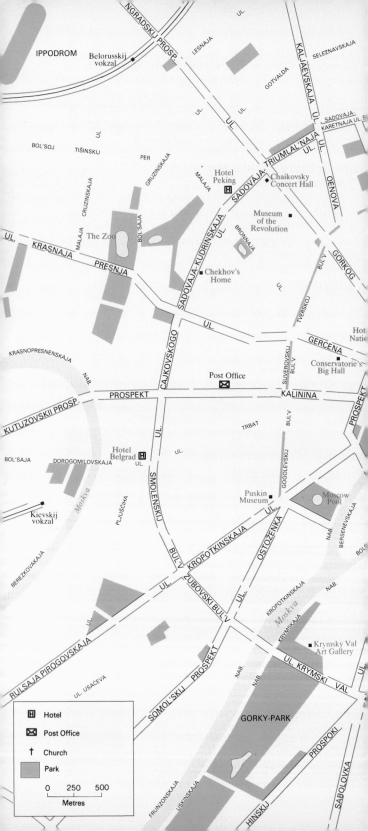

PROS

UL.

Olympic
Sports
Complex

GILJAROVSKOG

MIR

BOTANICAL
GARDENS

KALANOEV

VERHNJAJA KRASNOSEL'SKAJA UL.

Jaroslavskij
vokzal

OLIMPIJSKIJ

PROSPEKT

Kaločěvskaja

Leningradskij
vokzal

KRASNOPRUDNAJA

UL.

SADOVAJA-
SUHAREVSKAJA UL.

NAJA
UL.

SADOVAJA-

NOVOKIROVSKIJ
PROS

Hotel
Leningradskaya

LOVOT

JAZANSKAJA

UL.

SVJATOJ
BUL'V

SKIJ

SRETENKA

SPASSKAJA UL.

KIROVA

UL. KARLA MARKSA

ROZDESTVENSKIJ
BUL'V

UL.

SRETENSKIJ
BUL'V

ČISTOPUDNYJ
BUL'V

KAZAKOVA

DZERZINSKOGO

UL.

UL.

Moscow Central
Department Store

re

SA

OKTJABRJA

UL.

ČERNISEVSKOGO

UL.

KUJBYSEVA

POKROVSKIJ
BUL'V

ČKALOVA

Kurskij
vokzal

Red
quare

n

RAZINA

UL. SOLJANKA

† St Basil's
Cathedral

JAUZSKIJ
BUL'V

NOVSKAJA
NAB.

RAUSSKAJA

NAB.

SEREBRJANIČESKAJA
Jauza

NAB.

NIKOLOJAMSKAJA

NAB.

SADOVNIČESKAJA

NAB.

UL'JANOVSKAJA

UL.

BOLSAJA ORAVNKA

OZERKOVSKAJA

M. GORKOGO

UL.

LAGANSKAJA

VORONCOVSKAJA

BOL'SAJA ANDRONEVSK.

NOVOKUZNECKAJA

NAB.

KRASNOHOLMSKAJA

UL.

UL.

UL.

UL. ZEEPEKIJ VAL

SLJUZOVAJA

SARINSKIJ

SIMONOVSKIJ VAL.

DUBROVSKAJA

VALOVAJA

UL.

NAB.

Paveleckij
vokzal

UL.

1-JA

DUSINOVSKAJA

DUBININSKAJA

DERBENEVSKAJA

KRUTICKAJA

NAB.

UL.

PART III
Accommodation

Lobby of Mezhdunarodnaya Hotel

HOTELS

General Notes

Most hotels in the Soviet Union are run by **Intourist**. Their ratings, 'Top Class', 'Category 1', or 'Category Higher B', seem to be quixotic according to western standards. Also, the accommodations within the various categories may be quite different. The entire hotel industry in the USSR is geared to group tours and it is important to understand that. If you have small complaints that the friendly lady in charge of your floor can hadle you will find that she is willing to do so.

For more serious complaints go directly to your temporary godfather, your tour leader. Dining room woes are more difficult. Be firm. Patience, politeness and persistence are required.

All hotels have Beriozka shops of varying quality. See SHOPPING. Each hotel also has a currency exchange office and an Intourist Service Desk. Here all touring problems theoretically can be solved. Intourist arranges transportation, makes restaurant reservations, gets tickets and helps with all sightseeing.

The voltage of most hotels is 200 and European-type plugs fit into slanted sockets. Some rooms have colour television and the 'de luxe' rooms have a refrigerator. The hotel staff will gladly help if you run out of beverages to stock it. Several hotels have slot machines. If your idea of a sauna is a room with red-hot rocks and birch branches for beating, are you in for a surprise! Here the hotel saunas have bars and television.

There are few single rooms, they are available upon demand only with a hefty supplement in payment. On the other hand, folding cots for children are provided in the parents room (one child per adult) at 25 per cent reduction. There are also seasonal reductions at hotels except at certain health spas.

Most tours also include the price of meals. It is inconvenient to have to return to the hotel for them (inquire about meal vouchers) but it is usually preferable, except on excursions, to return rather than take the time to get in a crowded restaurant. **Breakfast** is usually a very large meal with everything except a dry cereal. Both the tea and coffee are excellent although you will have to 'make loud noises' to get a second cup of coffee!

The new **Savoy Hotel**, formerly the Berlin (and before that the Savoy) opened last year and is the most luxurious and decorated hotel in Moscow. Primarily for

Browsing in Arbat Street

businessmen, it offers full secretarial and communications services. Not an Intourist hotel, it is a joint Soviet-Finnair operation, reservations usually filled by Finnair customers.

There is a severe hotel shortage in the Soviet Union although new ones are constantly being built including some controlled by Aeroflot for intransit passangers. In general, most of them are hideous, a result of 'thinking big'. **The Cosmos**, one of the world's largest hotels, built for the 1980 Olympics, looks impressive from the outside. The lobby contains a hanging sculpture that looks exactly

like a collection of bent bicycle rims welded into a globe. Its twenty six storeys loom over, and completely overwhelm, a **statue of Peace** given to the Soviet Union by Greece.

In one hand it holds an olive branch, in the other a white dove. A plaque written in Russian and Greek has a wonderful quotation taken from Herodotus:

'No one can be so foolish as to want war instead of peace because when there is peace children bury their fathers, but in war fathers bury their children'.

HOTELS & NEAREST METRO STATIONS

ALTAI
41, Botanicheskaya St.
VDNKh

AEROFLOT
37, Leningrad Ave.
Dynamo Aeroport

BELGRADE 1
5, Smolenskaya Square
Smolenskaya

BELGRADE 2
8, Smolenskaya Square
Smolenskaya

BUDAPEST
2, Petrovskie Linii
Prospekt Marksa
Kuznetsky Most

KIEVSKAYA
2, Kievskaya Street
Kievskaya

KOSMOS
150, Mir Ave.
VDNKh

LENINGRADSKAYA
21, Kalanchevskaya St.
Komsomolskaya

MEZHDUNARODNAYA
12, Krasnopresnenskaya Em.
Ulitsa 1905 Goda

METROPOL
Sverdlov Square
Ploshchad Revolutsii
Prospekt Marksa

MINSK
22, Gorky Street
Mayakovskaya
Gorkovskaya
Punshkinskaya

MOLODEZHNAYA
27, Dmitrov Highway
Novoslobodskaya

MOSKVA
7, Marx Avenue
Prospekt Marksa
Ploshchad Revolutsii

NATIONAL
14, Marx Avenue
Prospekt Marksa

ORLENOK
15, Kosygin Street
Sportivnaya

DRUZHBA
53, Vernadsky Ave.
Prospekt Vernadskogo

INTOURIST
3, Gorky Street
Prospekt Marksa

IZMAILOVO
69, Izmailovskoye Highway
Izmailovsky Park

BUKHAREST
1, Sadovnicheskaya Emb.
Novokuznetskaya

MIR
9, Bolsoi Devyatinsky L.
Krasnopresnenskaya
Barrikadnaya

Mansion from 1820's

PART IV
Practical Information

PRACTICAL INFORMATION

A-Z Summary

The Building of TACC

СТОП

ADVANCE PLANNING

A visit to the Soviet Union can not be a 'causual affair'. Because of the special conditions in Russia one must plan very carefully in advance. For example, getting a visa can take three months, although when travelling with a tour this is cut down to two weeks. *No visa is issued without a hotel reservation.*

Every tourist activity is controled by **Intourist** in so far as documents, hotel reservations (rooms are scarce), and some tours are concerned. For this reason your trip to the USSR should start with a visit to an Intourist office if there is one in your area, and then to your travel agent.

Once in the Soviet Union, except for a few restricted areas, one is completely free to go where one wishes. The close constraints of pre-glasnost no longer exist.

> **INFOTIP:** To save time and money, plan your sightseeing around the opening and closing days of the places you wish to see, using your arrival and departure days for a museum or site that requires a short time. To avoid criss-crossing the vast areas of Moscow, group those items on your list which are near each other so that they can be covered in one jaunt.

What to bring

Documents
Passport, visa (separate from your passport) credit cards and once there, carry your hotel registration card with you.

Clothing
Russia is a casual country, however, as most other places, or perhaps more than other places, a well-dressed individual commands more respect. Casual clothing by all means, but don't try wearing very skimpy clothing or shorts outside the resort areas. Moscow is very warm in the summer but a light raincoat is a good idea because there are always unexpected rain showers, especially in July and August. It starts getting cool after the middle of August and for anytime after that it is good idea to dress like an onion, in other words, clothing that you can add and peel off in layers.

Winters are cold with lots of slush in the streets. The Metro and all public buildings (but not the museums!) are well heated. Sensible shoes are essential. Moscow streets and sidewalks are asphalt and therefor easy to walk on, but the distances are great, so comfort, not fashion, is the way to happiness here.

Practical Information

Entry Regulations
No one is allowed entry without a passport, a visa and a hotel reservation. Visas are issued according to length of stay and area visited but in emergencies (such as sudden illness) easily extended.

Special visas are granted for study, participation in seminars, exhibitions or for health treatments. Visas are not stamped in your passport.

Transit visas are also granted for explicit times and areas. These can not be extended. Aeroflot also makes arrangements for cheap transit visas of 72 hours duration which are available in Russia. Visas are not required for tourists travelling in cruise ships providing they are part of the tour.

Customs

Concessions for all Travellers
No Soviet currency may be imported, nor firearms, and certainly not drugs. Personnal effects such as cameras, et cetera should be declared for re-export. One litre of spirits and 250 cigarettes are officially allowed. It is also officially frowned on to carry in anything for third parties.

> **INFOTIP:** Except for cigarettes, which are very expensive at the Beriozka shops, there is no need to stock up on common requirements which are readily available and modestly priced in the large hard-currency stores. Do take a supply of toiletries and any medicines you will need during your stay. Perfume and cosmetics are available, but probably not your favourite brands. Also stock up on paper tissues. The famed toilet tissue shortage is not prevelent in the hotels, but there are no Kleenex or even napkins.

Tourist and Residents

Sweeping new regulations have just come into force regarding customs laws for citizens of the USSR as well as tourits. *'The new rules and customs duty rates go for Soviet and foreign citizens, as well as persons without citizenship coming to the USSR or leaving it for any purpose'*. The changes allow far more generous imports without duties, including cars, which now are charged only 33 per cent. Duties on almost everything else have been reduced as well. In reading between the lines, it would seem that the new policy is aimed at getting as much consumer goods into the USSR as quickly as possible.

> **INFOTIP:** The shortage of paper products is so accute that the cardboard backs from imported calendars are cut off to be used for other purposes.

Duty free

You can take anything you are able to carry out of the duty free shop. The excange of hard currency for souvenirs is enthusiastically applauded, however, objects considered to be part of the cultural or historic heritage can be exported by special permit only and they are subject to payment of custom duties equal to their value.

Pets

Even in Moscow one sees a few cats and many dogs of all sizes, but mainly large ones with lots of hair! Pets have entry in the USSR with the proper health certificates. You might like to know that the dogs in Moscow look happy!

Kransa (Red) Gate

Getting to Moscow

By Air: Aeroflot now serves almost every country in the world and is constantly making new agreements with other airlines. In some cases **LOT** (Polish Airlines) is an attractive alternative if you are eager to save money. Aeroflot does have charter flights. It also offers winter reductions and it can offer transit visas and accommodation. Always Check!

By Rail: Entry to the USSR by rail can start at any one of at least fifty major cities. The same general entry requirements apply. It is cheaper to start your journey from a Socialist country. See also GETTING OUTSIDE OF MOSCOW.

By Sea: Cruise ships are a major attraction for tourists who have the time and wish to tavel in luxury. There are many routes with varying time schedules. Visas are required for those wishing to leave the ship and extend their tour. For cruise details visit your local Intourist and your travel agent.

By Car: For many reasons travelling to Russia in your own, or even a rented vehicle is not practical. The distances alone are daunting and the problems of restrictions, regulations, visas and permissions are not really worth the hassle.

For Young Travellers

The Soviet Youth Organization, **SPUTNIK**, has contacts with other youth organizations all over the world and gladly arranges tours for them whenever a fair, exhibition, festival or whatever is going on. Through SPUTNIK your club or organization can get fare reductions as much as 50 per cent and you are guaranteed special treatment. There couldn't be a better way to spend any holiday!

> **INFOTIP:** The Sheremetyevo 2 Airport is one of the growing number with a duty free shop on arrival. It is fully stocked with all the items you would normally buy before arrival so you don't have to crowd your space with extra bags. If you are a smoker, buy cigarettes, they are expensive in the Beriozka shops. It is on the right before entering customs clearance.

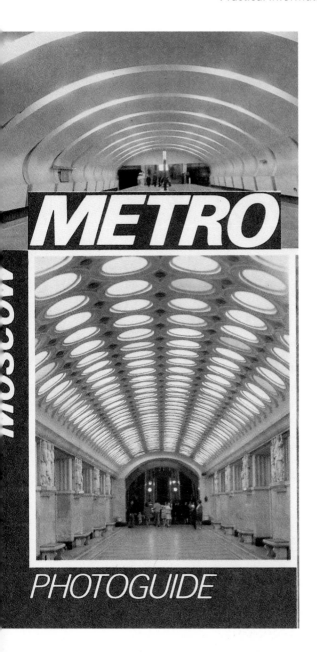

METRO

MOSCOW

PHOTOGUIDE

Electricity

In the hotels the standard is 220 volts, 50 cycles. Sockets are of the European type, plug pins are round. A continental plug adaptor, and a small transformer will be required for small appliances using 120 volts.

Entertainment

Tourists never need complain about a lack of entertainment in Moscow. All the major hotels have restaurants, discos, bars, floor shows or dancing. There is the ballet, circuses, concert halls theatres and all the many sports arenas, festivals and exhibitions all year long.

The new hotel Savoy even has the only casino in Russia, if you feel lucky. The real problem is getting in!

Reservations must be made in advance for almost everywhere you want to go, is better if you make them uppon your arrival. This can be done through your hotel **Intourist Service**.

Currant events are listed in the free handouts available and in '*Your guide in and around Moscow*'. Listings for all these appear under their own headings or with the hotel listings. Restaurants appear under 'Food'.

Circus

Moscow has two circuses, one often traveling. As always, the animal acts are superb. Not only the performances of the animals themselves will delight you, but the displays of horsemanship by troops from the various republics are unforgettable.

Entrance is impossible without reservations.

New Circus: Vernadskogo Prospect 17, Metro Universitet.
Old Circus: Tsvetnoy Bulvar 13, Metro Kolkoznaya.

Theatre and Ballet

The list below includes most of the major theatres although there are many smaller ones and many amatuer groups.

Kremlin Palace of Congresses: The Kremlin.
Tel. 226-79-90.
Bolshoi Opera & Ballet Theatre: 1 Sverdlov Sq.
Tel. 292-62-22.
Theatre of Friendship of the Peoples of USSR: 22 Tverskoy Boulevard. Tel. 203-62-22.
Moscow Academic Art Theatre: 3 Proyezd Khudozhestvennogo Teatra.
Art Theatre Branch: 3 Moskvin St. Tel. 229-96-31.
Maly Theatre: 1/6 Sverdlov Sq. Tel. 924-40-83.
Malu Theatre Branch: 69 Bolshaya Ordynka St.
Tel. 237-28-91.
Yevgeny Vakhtangov Drama Theatre: 26 Arbat St.
Tel. 241-07-28.
Mossoviet Theatre: 16 Bolshaya Sadovaya St.
Tel. 299-20-35.
Stanislavsky & Nemirovich-Danchenko Musical Theatre:
17 Pushkinskaya St. Tel. 229-83-88.
Central Children's Theatre: 2 Sverdlov Sq. Tel. 292-00-69.
Children's Musical Theatre: 5 Vernadsky Prospekt.
Tel. 130-51-77.
Gogol Drama Theatre: 8a Kazakov St. Tel. 261-55-28.
Malaya Bronnaya Drama Theatre: 4 Malaya Bronnaya St.
Tel. 290-04-82.
New Drama Theatre: 2 Prokhodchikov St. Tel. 182-03-47.
Pushkin Drama Theatre: 23 Tverskoy Boulevard.
Tel. 203-42-21.
Moscow Regional Drama Theatre: 9,25th October St.
Tel. 925-10-44
Yermolova Drama Theatre: 5 Gorky St. Tel. 203-79-52
Durov Animal Theatre: 4 Durov St. Tel. 971-30-47
Lenin Komsomol Theatre: 6 Chekhov St. Tel. 299-96-68
Mime Theatre: 39/4 Izmailovsky Boulevard. Tel. 163-81-30
Miniature Theatre: 3 Karetny Ryad St. Tel. 209-20-76
Satiricon Theatre: 8 Sheremetyevskaya St. Tel. 289-79-44
Soviet Army Theatre: 2 Commune Sq. Tel. 281-51-20
Roman Gypsy Theatre: 32 Leningradsky Prospekt.
Tel. 250-73-34
Variety Theatre: 24 Bersenevskaya Embankment.
Tel. 230-04-44
Young Spectators Theatre: 10 Sadovsky Lane.
Tel. 299-86-85

Tranquility in Moscow

Parks and Gardens

Moscow's parks and gardens are a combination of restful places to stroll and areas of entertainment. Many feature placid lakes, roisterous Luna Parks, bandstands, concert halls, and even small theatres. There are exhibitions, dancing and of course, restaurants, cafes and snack bars.

Izmailovo Recreation Park: 17 Narodny Prospekt.
Sokolniki Recreation Park: 1 Sokolnichesky Val.
Botanical Gardens of the USSR, Academy of Science: 4 Botanicheskaya Street.
Moscow Univercity Botanical Gardens: Lenin Hills.
Druzhba Forest Park: 90 Leningradskoye Highway.
Kuskovo Forest Park: 40, 3rd Muzeinaya Street.
Serebryany Bor Forest Park: Serebryany Bor, 1st Line.
Hermitage Garden: 3 Karetny Ryad Street.

Casino

Gambling has arrived in Russia by way of the Casino in the Hotel Savoy, the only Casino in Russia. Hard currency only is accepted, preferably credit cards. Only foreigners are allowed to play and whereas gambling losses are to be paid immediately, winnings are paid by marker, collectable outside Russia!

Cinema

As of this writing there are no foreign films being shown with original soundtracks or foreign sub-titles, although there are various weeks of foreign film festivals. Most offerings are Soviet or from Socialist countries and, up to now, dull! A new wave of realizm and docu-drama films have become popular. Soviet film goers would like to see more westerns, horror films and those the western film critics complain are too full of violence, mainly because they would be such a novelty!

Television/Video/Radio

Television

There are four channels in colour, but two or three of them are frequently running the same programme which often consists of hours-long historical Russian movies. Also very big is State projects featuring interviews with workers in construction, mining, et cetera.

Classical music and concerts, disco and even rock music seem to be standard fare. Language lessons in French, English and German are popular along with children's programmes and excellent cartoons. There seems to be an emphasis on ethnic folk dancing but some foreign news clips are also shown.

Video

There is a flourishing black market in video tapes, American Westerns are much in demand. Only blank video tapes can be brought into the Soviet Union. There are video tapes for sale to tourists. The pro-reform magazine, 'Ogonyok' even produces its own news series, but it is not allowed to advertise the tapes in its own pages.

Radio

Both the BBC and the Voice of America broadcast the news and the Russian Moscow Service is also in English.

Currency

The Russian den'gi (200-1 rouble) and the givna (20 den'gi) are gone, but the kopek, 100 to the rouble, still comes in metal coins of 1,2,3,5,10,,15,20 and 50 kopek pieces.

> **INFOTIP:** Always keep several small coins for telephone calls, Metro and Bus fares. Don't be surprised if, on the street, you are occasionally asked for 2 kopeks for a telephone call.

The paper rouble comes in denominations of 1,3,5,10,25,50 and 100 in notes. There are also many special commemorative one rouble coins in circulation to gladden a collector's heart, and they are often given as change.

Furtive characters flit about hotels and in the streets offering to buy dollars at 10-15 times the official rate. In addition to being strictly illegal, such excanges can be risky and dangerous since the age-old trick of topping counterfeit bills with a few genuine has not lost its appeal. The 'kedali' offer even more but they work in pairs and while one is giving you the bargain of a life time the other is waiting down the street to robe you. See also PART V BUSINESS GUIDE.

Monument to Space Conquerers

Festivals & Public Holidays

Moscow sponsors two large art festivals during the year. '**Moscow Stars**' (May) and '**Russian Winter**' (Dec.-Jan.). The finest professional and amateur companies from all over the Soviet Union gather here to perform in a spectacular series of shows.

These include theatrical productions, outdoor concerts and performances in many different surroundings. The 'Russian Winter' includes troika rides, ice skating and hot blinis and caviar with the New Year's Festivities. The troika rides are at the flea market (Izmailovo Park), Gorky Park and at the Exhibition Achievments.

Art & Folk Festivals

December/January
Russian Winter
Art, Moscow. Folk, Moscow, Vladimir, Suzdal, Novgorod, Irkutsk.

March
Mertsishor
Art, Kishinev.
Farewell to Russia Winter
Folk, Moscow, Suzdal.
Navruz
Folk, Dushanbe
Festival of the North
Folk, Murmansk.

April
Festival devoted to the birth-anniversary of Vladimir Lenin.
Art, Ulyanovsk.
Arts Day
Folk, Riga.

May
Moscow Stars
Art, Moscow.
Kiev Spring
Art, Kiev
Red Carnation
Ivanovo.

June
White Nights
Art, Leningrad
Ligo
Folk, Riga

The Cosmos Pavilion

July
Baltika
Art, Vilnius

August
Sorochintsy Fair
Art, Poltava Region, Village of Sorochintsy.

September
Handicrafts Days
Art, Vilnius

October
Tbilisoba
Art, Tbilisi

November
Byelorussian Musical Autumn
Art, Minsk

Public Holidays

1 January	New Year's Day
8 March	International Women's Day
1 May	International Working People's Solidarity Day
9 May	Victory Day, in memory of the great Patritic War of 1941-1945
7 October	USSR Constituition Day
7 November	Anniversary of the 25th October 1917 Socialist Revolution
27 September	World Tourism Day

Moscow's Underground Map

Getting Around Moscow

Buses: Put 5 kopeks in tellar, take ticket and keep for the duration of your ride. Ten-ride carnets cost 50 kopeks and can be purchased from the driver between stops and at some underpass entrances. Stamp the ticket yourself at one of the small machines positioned through the bus at eye level on the windows. It is perforated by pushing the knob. Sometimes in a crowded bus, if you are near a machine, others will hand you a ticket to punch.

Taxis: Every taxi is easily recognizable and you can get one from a hotel taxi stand, have your hotel call one or hail a taxi on the street. Every taxi has a meter and is supposed to charge 20 kopeks per kilometer with 20 already on the meter. Practically speaking, any ride will cost at least 2 roubles. Many drivers speak English and it is always advisable to agree on the fare before getting in, overcharge in this profession knows no politics nor any frontiers!

Beware especially of taxis hanging around hotels and famous tourists spots like the Kremlin. Always negotiate before getting in, even Russian's often refuse their demands. Don't be surprised if while hailing a cab a private car swoops down on you. These 'pirates' often charge less, at least no more, but they do charge. They are a welcome sight at rush hours!

Taxi-Bus: These are mini-buses which move along fixed routes of which there are thirty-six. The official price is 15 kopeks regardless of length of ride, but some ask double the price. You can get out anywhere along the way by requesting the driver to stop.

> **INFOTIP:** Before setting out to any destnation, by whatever means, have someone write the address in Russian for you. This can save much time and many misunderstandings.

River Trams: From May to September or October (depending on the weather) large boats with open decks and below-deck glassed-in salons travel up and down the Moskva River three times a day. The terminals are the International Trade Center and the Novospassky Bridge. The entire trip takes about 2.00 hours. Along the way one can see many of the famous buildings of Moscow and get an entirely different perspective of this busy metropolis.

Hydrofoil: If you are in a hurry you can ride the Raketa or Meteor hydrofoils which travel from Gorky Park to the Novospassky Bridge then to Kievsky Vokzal Pier. These two hydrofoils also serve the express lines of the Northern and Southern River Terminal which harbour the double and triple decker river boats linking Moscow to the Baltic, Black, White caspian Seas and the Sea of Azov.

The Metro: The Moscow Metro deserves its world wide reputation for cleanliness, swiftenss, convenience and beauty. First proposed in 1902, it was rejected as being to disrupting to the peace and quiet of the city and too dangerous for the building foundations.

It finally opened on May 15, 1935 along tracks stretching 11.6 kilometers. Soon it was carrying 350.000 passengers, now its 132 stations service eight million passengers daily. During the rush hours 43 eight car trains traveling at 70 kms per hour, arrive at intervals of between 60-90 seconds at every station.

Use of the Metro is so much of Moscow's life that almost all locations are identified by the nearest Metro station.

Each station is built in a different style, reflecting either the era in which it was built or the architectural style of the era around the entrance.

Some of the most famous stations are: **Ploshchad Revolutsii**, with a total of 76 bronze statues of professional and military figures. **Komsomolskaya** is the largest and features traditional styles of Russian architecture and paintings. Named after a poet, the **Mayakovskaya** Station was awarded the Grand Prix at the World's Fair in 1937, decorated with mosaic panels and its columns are stainless steel faced with the rare mineral, radonite.

Cost of tickets: The Metro costs only 5 kopeks, but you can buy a card which also happens to be good for all the buses. A card costs 2 roubles for ten days, 3 for 15 days and 6 roubles for a month. The cards are also good for trams and trolleys although they do not have to be shown when entering.

> **INFOTIP:** Despite its complexity, the Metro is easy to use and most tourist sites list the nearest Metro Station. A photoguide with pictures of most of the Metro stations is available from Planeta Publishers.

Moscow River Harbour

Getting Outside of Moscow

Trains: Every day 3.700 local and long distance trains carrying 2 million passengers arrive and depart from Moscow stations. There are nine separate railway stations serving routes of varying lengths. Many of the trains are express serving the capitals of the republics and all the larger cities. It is sometimes faster to go by train than to fly. The '**Aurora**' express train which goes between Moscow and Leningrad takes only five hours whereas counting check-in time, et cetera, flying can take up to seven hours. You also have the advantage of seeing some of the beautiful countryside along the way, or of saving hotel expenses for one evening if you travel by night. These trains all have dining cars but it is not a bad idea to take your own snacks and liquid refreshments along.

The **Trans-Siberian Railway** takes passangers from Europe to the Pacific on the world's longest continuous journey, 6.000 miles. There are many stops along the way and at various locations **Intourist** arranges excursions to the most scenic areas.

A new Trans-Siberian Express will soon start service from Paris to Vladivostok. In addition to luxurious passenger cars it will carry a sauna and two dining cars. Along some streches the train will be pulled by steam locomotives and, to enchance the turn-of-the-century

Station Polshad Revoloutsyi

mood, the conductors will wear uniforms similar to those worn when the coaches wore the double-headed eagle emblem of the Tsars!

By Air: In keeping with statistics concerning the Soviet Union, it can be said that **Aeroflot** is the largest airline in the world and the one with the largest cargo capacity. It now carries 115 million passengers a year, but by using the most capitalist method of advertising, it hopes to greatly increase that number. The Moscow terminal at International Sheremebyevo 2 (1 is domestic) is but one of the 3.600 airports in the Soviet Union.

Aeroflot also flies to 125 cities in 98 countries and has reciprocal agreements with many of these, one of which is Pan Am. The two airlines have a joint booking office SPATE, through which agents can book hotel rooms in downtown Moscow.

From Europe the shortest route to Japan is the **Trans-Siberian Route** over the North Pole, and it is three hours quicker.

Aeroflot has now joined IATA, which will bring its regulations in line with other carriers.

> **INFOTIP:** Aeroflot is very generous, with its luggage allowance when flying out of the country and it serves ample meals. Caviar anyone?

Help!

Embassies

Various functions of most embassies are housed in separate compounds, therefore it is best to call before going. Both the American and British commercial departments are not on the grounds of the Embassy and for this reason have easier access. The French Embassy is in a beautiful building, a tourist attraction itself because it was built in the old style of Russian architecrure. the new American Embassy is only partly functioning. The interference on Embassy telephone lines is usually quite bad.

United Kingdom, Tel. 231 8511
United States, Tel. 252 2451
Canada, Tel. 241 5882

For lisiting of more Embassies contact the Intourist Services Desk.

Medical Services

Hotel guests may call the Intourist Service Desk and obtain first aid free of charge. Hospitalization is billed, but the charges are reasonable. Should your illness require a longer stay Intourist will arrange an extension of your visa and tour.

Spas and Doctors

There are many famous spas all over the Soviet Union and several well known specialty clinics in Moscow which cater to foreigners. People come for treatment from all over the world. Many Soviet doctors have developed treatments which either can not be found in other countries or are cheaper here.

One of the better known, which advertises more vigorously than any Western organization, made even more famous by international television, is the **Fyodorov Clinic**. Under the slogan, '*Beautiful Eyes for Everybody*', and with the state aim of completely eliminating eye glasses, Dr Fyodorov's remarkable center for eye microsurgery performs operations for cornea transplants, cataract extractions, silicone implants and, a highly controversial, but very successful, system of 'conveyer belt' patients.

By this method as many as 150 operations per day are performed by five different surgeons who each specialize in a separate phase of the operation, the most difficult part of the operation performed by the most skilled surgeon. Over 25.000 operations with a success rate of 97 per cent (restoring visual acuity 70-100 per cent, official figures), have already been performed for treatment of cataracts, glaucoma and myopia.

The most popular treatment involves myopia surgery (technically known as radial keratotomy). Most people, as they get older, suffer either from long-sightedness (myopia) of short-sightedness (hyperopia). Both of these afflictions are cured by making corneal incisions, a method first tried in Japan by Dr. Sato. Although his method was a failure, the idea was sound, and by making changes in the operation it has now become a success.

In general the cost of treatment, which includes laser, reconstruction surgery, et cetera are very reasonable. At present general examination costs $100 US, an eye operation $750 US and the daily hospital charge is $40 US. During hospitalization one can still go sightseeing, which certainly makes surgery here even more economical.

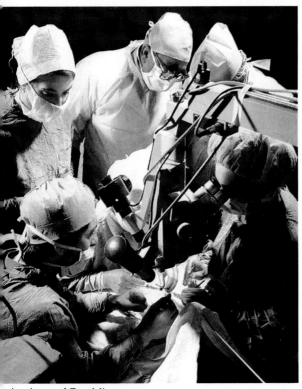

Institute of Eye Micro surgery

Other Emergencies

For any emergencies contact the Intourist Desk at your Hotel, or phone Intourist Moscow 292-2260, they are at 16 Marx Prospekt, Moscow 1030099, there is another office at 1 Gorky Street.

St. Saviour Tower - its clock and chimes

> **INFOTIP:** Inquires can be made to: Foreign trade Company, 'Eye Micro-Surgery' 59A Beskudnikovsky Blvd. Moscow 127486 USSR. Telex 411856 OKO. Tel. 484 8120.

Crime

Moscow is safer than most cities elsewhere. But here, as anywhere else, one can't do stupid things like prowling around dark streets at night. In addition to the harmless '**Irons**', who only want to sell your western clothing to other young Russians like themselves, there are the '**Kendali**', these are young punks who are into minor crimes like black marketing and petty theft.

Despite denials from the government, there are drug problems, but this nowhere approaches the pandemic proportions of the West.

Believe it or not most of the petty street crime is done out of sheer boredom. If city authorities would allow private enterprise to take over the entertainment gap much of this problem would be solved.

Motoring

Private Cars

There use to be many restrictions imposed on drivers of private cars, but now most restrictions are eased. With so many changes going on it is best to check current regulations with Intourist. Of course the usual requirements of visa, passport, et cetera still apply. Besides having all the proper documents for the car you must also have a stamp of the hotel or motel at your first stopping place on your visa. Driving is on the right.

Hired Cars

These are available, through Intourist!, with or without a chauffeur, the price includes insurance, maintenance costs and maps showing motels and camping grounds. Order through your hotel Intourist Service Desk or at the hotel Cosmos, Tel. 215-6191.

Publications in English

Newspaper

In the new spirit of 'glasnost' news is now easy to get. The printed world, particularly interesting, and for Russia, radical comments, is found in the **Moscow News**. This newspaper is printed all over the world but until a few years ago, ignored in Moscow, however, its editorial policy changed and it has since become very popular. Moscovites rush out at six in the morning to buy a copy before it is sold out.

Called 'radical' because it tells the truth, the Moscow News, in its English editions, is a fascinating glimpse of life in Russia as it is today.

Bookshops

One of the delights of Moscow is the huge number and variety of bookshops. In the larger ones beautiful art books are found in several languages, including English books in many fields and many English editions of the works of the most famous Russian authors.

They also sell maps, postcards, stamps and they have an excellent selection of calendars, both Russian and imported, with Russian and English texts. In the summer one can also find posters, for the following year, of great beauty and propaganda some hysterically funny.

All of the Beriozska shops have a good section of art books sold for hard currency only. Prices are steep but most of these can not be obtained in Russian or hotel bookshops which sell in roubles.

Books, 8/10 Vesnin St. Metro Smolenskaya. Park Kultury.
Dom Knigi, 26 Prospekt Kalinia.(Moscow's largest bookshop)
Book World, Kirova Ulitsa 6.
Druzhba, 15 Gorky Street.
Moskva, 8 Gorky Street.

> **INFOTIP:** The only bookshop in the Soviet Union which specializes in buying and selling used books in foreign languages has just opened. SECOND-HAND BOOKSHOP No 79 (inostrannaya Bukinistiche Kniga) at 16 Kashalo St. Sells antique books lithographs and maps in foreign languages.

Kremlin Palace of Congresses

Post Office

Letters within the USSR and to any of the Socialist countries cost 5 Kopeks, the envelope 1 kopek. Capitalist countries rate 50 kopeks,it is usual to buy stamped envelopes at kiosks.

Postcards cost 6 kopeks, postage 20. Don't expect free stationery at the hotel. Register airmail costs 1.05 roubles.

Every Intourist hotel has a post office and letters can be sent from there or the blue letter boxes standing outside.

Post Restante

The address is Hotel Intourist, K-600, 315 Ulitsa Gorkogo.

Parcels

These can be sent from the International Post Office at Varshavkoye Shosse 37, Tel. 111-1392.

Kadashevskaia embankment

Moscow in the 1920's-1930's

Philatelics

Hotels, bookstores and kiosks sell an incredible variety of beautiful stamps, miniature paintings really, which are so interesting one does not have to be a collector to enjoy them. Each year 100 new designs are issued and sold in sheets and folders. The collector's paradise is **Moskovsky Dom Knigi**, Prospekt Kalinina 26, Metro Arbatskaya.

Photography

There is much you will want to film (one sees many video cameras) so take more film than you think you will need, especially because it can not be processed inside the USSR so you will want to take back-up shots. Also take along as many batteries as your electronic equipment will need.

Do not attempt to film anything that could be construed as being of military interest, keep your cameras in your hand luggage at airports.

Pack films to avoid the possibility of damage by x-ray machines. There are many camera shops in Moscow but the large Beriozka shops have a better selection of photo equipment, including video cameras.

Religious Services

There are many operating churches in and around Moscow that can be visited during services. Glowing candles reflecting in the gold of the altar and other precious church appointments, shoot off sparks from the gems in the sacred ikons and give the scene an unearthly appearance. If you are lucky you will hear the majestic liturgy of the Russian Orthodox Church always sung a capella. Worshippers come and go but they do not disturb those who remain. Be unobtrusive and do not use your camera.

Church of the Assumption, 1 Novodevichy Proyezd.
The Church of the Transfiguration, 17 Krasnobogatyrskaya St.
The Trinity Church, Universitetskaya Sq. Lenin Hills.
The Church of St. John the Warrior, 46 Dimitrov St.
The Church of the Resurrection, 15/2 Nezhdanova St.
The Church of All Sorrowful, 20 Bolshaya Ordynka St.
The Church of All Saints, 73 Leningradsky Prospekt.
The Cathedral of the Epiphany in Yelokhovo,
15 Spartakovskaya St
The Greek Orthodox Church, 15a Telegraphy Lane.
St. Nicholas Unitarian Church, 1a/29 Rogozhsky Posyolok.
Old Believers Society, 29 Rogozhsky Posyolok.
The Church of the Assumption, 29 Volodarsky St
. Society of Evangelic Christian Baptists, 3 Maly Vuzovsky Lane.
Catholic Church, 12 Malaya Lubyanka St.
Choral Synagogue, 8 Arkhipov St.

Restaurants & Nightlife

Food and Drink

Although official Moscow guides boast of over nine thousand eating places from magnificent restaurants to humble schashlik grills, the truth is that other than hotels and restaurants, with reservations in advance, most tourists will have a hard time sampling all the delicious specialities Russia has to offer.

The famous **kvass**, which used to be a drink strained through spiced or rye bread, is alas, in the curbside version, tasteless. But try it! Most of the ice cream, on the other hand, is delicious and is sold on the street, everywhere. It can even be bought in Bricks to take home.

INFOTIP: Sometimes Russians just squeeze a few drops of lemon juice over it as a topping, its delicious.

Holy Gospel, The Armoury Chamber

Some of the Beriozka shops have a mini-supermarket and the ones at **Hotel Rossiya** and the **Hotel Mezhdunarodnaya** (International Hotel) especially, have a wide selection of imported foods, frozen foods, snacks and even fresh vegetables. There also have cigarettes, soft drinks, beer and alcohol of all the familiar brands.

Included of course, is **caviar**. The best, grey, is reserved for government officials and the sports and ballet elite, but there are an abundance of the black pearls from Caspian sturgeon. The red roe of the salmon is also displayed in tiered rows of two ounce tins. Even here caviar is not cheap. Avoid buying it in glass, the tinned variety holds better. Only in the hotels do Russians serve caviar with hard-cooked eggs (it goes further!) since the best flavour is obtained by eating it 'straight', without lemon, but chilled. They do often serve it curled up in the famous **blinis** (pancakes), hot off the gridle.

Do try the **bread**. It is delicious and, government subsidized, ridiculously cheap. The lines move very quickly and its worth waiting for. Be on the lookout for the 'Borodin' bread which is very dark, heavy and soul satisfying. As of this writing there are no shortages of bread, milk or butter in Moscow. By the way, there is also a wide variety of delicious cakes and cookies which you should try as well.

The famous **Russian Vodka** is in short supply, always long lines for it, but there are many wines and brandies for sale. Sometimes there are sugar shortages due to the making of '*bathtub Vodka*'! The sugar soft drinks are better left undescribed, but there is always plenty of mineral water.

Mostly meals consist of four main course starting with appetizers then soup, entre and dessert served with a wide assortment of wines and finishing with tea or coffee. Typical Russian dishes include:

Bliny, a hot pancake wrapped around caviar and smothered with butter and sour cream or slathered with jam or honey.

Borsch, which can contain twenty ingredients other than beef.

Pelmeni, which is a Siberian specialty. These are meat dumplings hidden in dough and served floating in broth or garnished with any number of dressings. In Siberia, that gigantic free freezer, pelmeni are made by the sackful, kept frozen and served all winter in countless variations.

INFOTIP: In Russia, 'Russian Salad' is called 'sald Olivier', or 'Capital Salad' in honour of Moscow. Most of the cooking is done with sunflower oil. Olive oil is not available and corn is hard to find.

Church of the Deposition of the Holy Robe

Restaurants

Despite Moscow's well-advertised food shortages, there are many restaurants which serve delicious meals. Most are in the hotels, but more and more co-op places are opening serving full meals or teas. Each hotel generally has its own cuisine specializing in regional dishes.

For Russian's a restaurant meal means a 'night out'. In other words, they are there for the entire evening, don't expect quick service or a quickly vacated table. Meals are not cheap, between 30 and 50 roubles.

Make reservations through Intourist.

Practical Information

Arbat, 21 Kalinin Avenue. Enormous establishment with floor shows and dancing. Some of the many variety acts are amazing.

Starry Sky, 3 Gorky Street, at the Intourist Hotel has a large floor show and dancing.

Come and Taste, is locally a famous little place. It is a small basement restaurant with one of its rooms decorated in a Greek style since its owner is Greek.

Azerbaijanian Tea Shop, Zulbovsky Square, a quiet oasis facing a teeming avenue serving delicious tea and a variety of cakes. You might have the experience of being served by a delightful, but slightly tipsy, waiter!

Russian Cuisine
Minsk, 22 Gorky Street.
Moskva, 7 Marx Avenue.
Rossiya, 6 Razin Street.
Slavyansky Bazar, 17/25 Oktyabrya Street.
Tsentralny, 10 Gorky Street.

Georgian Cuisine
Aragvi, 6 Gorky Street.

Azerbaijanian Cuisine
Baku, 24 Gorky Street

Yugoslavian Cuisine
Belgrad, 5 and 8 Smolenskaya Square

Hungarian Cuisine
Budapest, 2 Petrovskie Linii

Indian Cuisine
Delhi, 23 Krasnaya Presnya Street

Vietnam Cuisine
Hanoi, 20, 60 Letiya Oktyabrya Avenue

Cuban Cuisine
Havana, 88 Lenin Avenue

Chinese Cuisine
Peking, 1 Bolshaya Sadovaya Street

Chech and Slovac Cuisine
Praga, 2 Arbat Street

Bulgarian Cuisine
Sofia, 32 Gorky Street

Ukrainian Cuisine
Ukraina, 2 Kutuzov Avenue

Uzbek Cuisine
Uzbekistan, 29 Neglinnaya Street

Polish Cuisine
Varshava, 2 Oktyabrskaya Square

Armenian Cuisine
Yerevan, 37 Yerevan Street

Fish Dishes
Yakor, 49 Gorky Street

Mayakovskaya Station

Interior of the Faceted Chamber

Cafes and Snack-Bars

There are no snack-bars or fast food chains where one can quickly get a hamburger or fish and chips. McDonald's, however, is now opening the largest of its establishments in the world , 900 seating capacity. Its first in Russia and situated at Gorky Street at Pushkin Square, will sell in roubles and the second in hard currency.

There are a few cafes and ice cream parlous, places to buy beer and very cheap cafeterias, a real experience, but these are always crowded, hard to find, and if on a busy schedule, not worth the effort.

One does see areas outside parks, Metro entrances and in the Exhibition grounds where snack type foods are sold along with the ever-popular ice cream.

Nightlife

Bars

All the tourist hotels have bars with varying hours of operation. The Cosmos hotel has a Hall-Bar open around the clock, but most close at 2am. Many of these are actually bar-restaurants.

Discos

As with every place of entertainment, there are long lines, especially since most open at 6pm and close at 11pm. There are mostly for students and young adults.

Russian Youth Center: Molodiozhny Tssentr. Metro Yugo-Zapadnaya. Bus 165, last stop.
Kafe 'Melelytsa': Kalininsky Prospekt 12. Metro Arbatskaya.
Sad Baumana: Karl Marx Prospekt 12. Sat. & Sun only.
Hotels: Cosmos, Izmailov, Mezhdounarodnaya. Roubles and hard currency only.

Celebration in Red Square

Shopping

In view of the much publized shortages in the Soviet Union you might be wondering what there is to buy. Rest assured that there is an abundance of beautiful and unique items beyond the ubiquitous and over priced **Matyoshka dolls**. Here one is overwhelmed by the craftsmanship of not one nation, but fifty Republics!

Wherever you buy, there is only one rule about shopping in the Soviet Union, if you see something you feel you realy can't live without, buy it then and there. This even applies to the booklets one finds in the bookshops and at various sites, because you may not see it again.

In Moscow every man, women and child wears a carry-all bag over the shoulder as all-pervasive as an elephant's trunk just in case something needed is suddenly available. Muscovites are constantly swooping down on a stand or counter just to see what is being sold, as just as quickly darting away again.

Beautiful Furs

Beriozka Shops

Unique to Socialist countries is the hard currency shop, known in the Soviet Union as the 'Beriozka Shps', the name means birchtree, which is as much a symbol of Russia as the bear. Prices are written in roubles but payment is only in Western currency.

These shops are different in one other respect too, they are the only ones to have electronic cash registars, all other shops still use the ancient but accurrate abacas!

They are run by Intourist and generally feature handicrafts, books, souvenirs and small items. The larger ones have everything from food to photographic equipment, cigarettes, beverages, even electronic equipment. As with any shopping, browse first. Keep the sales receipts for customs, although you probably will not be required to show them. All major credit cards are accepted.

Department Stores

These are invariably overcrowed. So much so that there are often long lines at various departments waiting until other shoppers leave. It is best to visit them early in the morning or an hour before closing time. They are usually open Monday to Saturday.

GUM, 3 Krasnaya Ploshchad (Red Square)
GUM is pronounce Goom
A fascinating building with many arcades and galleries. Don't be surprised if you offered, by free-lancers, various items including trendy Russian Army watches!

Detsky Mir, Prospekt Marksa 2
The world's largest department store for children.

Dom Igrushki, Kutuzovskiy Prospekt 8
House of toys and related items.

Central Department Store (TsUM), Petrovka Street 2

Moskva Department Store, Leninsky Prospekt 54

Specialties Stores

Yantar, Stoleshnikov Pereulok 13
Large selection of Amber.

Dom Farfora
The House of Porcelain, and the largest selection of Matryoshka Dolls. They come in many different designs and sets but those with as many as 13 within one another are too large to be 'cute'.

Co-op, Petrovka Ulitsa 16
Embroideries

State Store, corner of Petrovka & Stoleshnikov
Furs, beautiful, but no bargains.

Jewelry Almaz, State jeweler, Stolenshnikov 14
Diamonds.

Biryuza, Sadovaya-Spasskaya 21
Turquoise

Samotsvety, Arbat Street 35
Semi-precious stones.

Izumrud, Lomonosvsky Prospekt 23
Emeralds

Rubin, Leningradsky Prospekt 78
Rubies

INFOTIP: When buying at shops the normal procedure is to get a sales slip, take it to the cashier and return to the original counter. If you buying from several counters it is best to gather all the slips and pay them together.

Cigarettes

With western cigarettes so expensive in the Beriozska shops this might be the time to try Russian ones. The most unusual are the '**papirosi**', a short cigarette fitted into a long hollow tube. Russian tobacco, however, will seem harsh to those used to western blends. Cuban cigars are in good supply. Souvenir sets of match boxes are a good buy.

Farmer's Markets

Food for the average Soviet household is obtaind from three major sources: **Kolkhoz** (collective farm) where production targets are set and the workers, who share everything, are required to meet this target. Naturally, they also share in the proceeds of the total output.
Sovkhoz, a large state farming enterprise which is completely owned by the state and the workers are paid regular wages without sharing in the profits.
The third source is from **private plots of land**, each

around two acres, every kolkhoz worker is allowed to till along with raising small numbers of live stock. Food from these plots is generally of better quality but more expensive.

In visiting a farmer's market one sees the produce from all these sources and is able to compare the quality and the price.

Baumansky, 47/1 Baumansky Street.
Bolshoi Kolkhozny, 8 Khukhrikov Lane.
Cheryomushkinsky, 1 Lomonsovsky Pr.
Danilovsky, 78 Mytnaya Street
Rizhsky, 94/96 Pr. Mira.

Komsomolskaya Station

Flowers

Women selling flowers are at almost every Moscow Metro entrance and sybway crossing. According to the season one sees all the beautiful varieties and some that are unsual.

Have you ever seen a deep purple gladiola? They are also reasonable in price although it can be safely assumed the seller flew in with them from some distance.

Fashion

One does see, some well-dressed Moscovites who obviously are wearing clothes either from a co-op or made by a private tailor.

Fashion events are held in Moscow by Dior and Nina Ricci and Moscow's own fashion designer Vyacheslav Zaitsev.

Young people are mostly dressed in acid and stone-washed jeans, but everyone is curious to see what the well-dressed foreigner is wearing.

The women use a great deal of eye make-up wear nylons and pantyhose with fancy patterns and many are statuesque and stunning.

Flea Market

Yes, Moscow has a flea market, but it is comparatively new. On long paths one finds hundreds of the usual items and many for tourists as well.

Paintings, carvings, household knick-knacks, toys, jewelry and many versions of the famous Matryoshka dolls, some of them costing up to $1.000.

Makers of these dolls took full advantage of perestroika and created others which are caricatures of former leaders. There was for example a Brezhnev doll painted with representations of the many medals he loved to wear and inside were members of his cabinet, each succeding one with fewer medals.

Izmailovsky Park, Metro Izmaylovskaya, Sundays only.

INFOTIP: Official it is forbidden to carry anything into the Soviet Union SPECIFICALLY for third parties such as friends and relatives.

Moskvosky Dept. Store

Cruising Past the Kremlin

Telephone & Telegraph

For 2 kopeks one can call anywhere in Moscow from a puplic phone. A local call at your hotel is free. You can also call long distance almost anywhere by booking in advance. Dial 8-194. Calls to Europe cost 3 roubles per minute, to the USA, 6 roubles per minute.

A **telegraph** can be sent by calling 927-2002. They can also be send from any post office. *The Central Telegraph is on Ulitsa Gorkogo 7, Metro Prospekt Marksa.*

Time

Moscow time is Greenwich time plus 3 hours. Noon in London is 3pm in Moscow. Savings time adds another hour from the end of March to the end of September. As you know, there are a total of 11 time zones in the Soviet Union, from east to west.

Tipping

One of the prospects of Socialism is that tipping is degrading to the recipient. This feeling has long since passed with the influx of foreigners, many of whom never felt degraded at home when receiving tips for their services!

Fortunately, small tips are still accepted in the Soviet Union with a smile instead of a snear, 5 to 10 per cent is fine. If during your stay you think you have recieved service above and beyond duty, you might like to give something extra, here are a few ideas for small items more valuable than money:

Chewing gum and candy bars for children. Small cannisters of tea or coffee, pantyhose for women, briefs for men, western cigarettes, French perfume. All these can be bought in the Berizka shops. Also be sure that good use can be made of fairly new used clothing you wish to leave behind.

Sports Facilities

Bowling

Hotel Cosmos

Saunas

Hotel Cosmos
Hotel Sevastopol
Hotel Solnechny (sauna and bar)
Hotel Mozhaisky (closed on Sundays)

Swimming Pools

Hotel Cosmos

Note: Most hotels are constantly updating their facilities. The Hotel Savoy is planning a complete health club. Check with INTOURIST.

Toilets

Public toilets, some of them privately maintained, are easily recognizable (but hard to find) because they often have W.C written along the Russian word. Fees are from 10-20 kopeks, the price has nothing to do with the quality of the facility.

Water

Bottled mineral water is sold but the tap water is perfectly safe to drink, and is very soft. Laundry needs little soap.

Intourist

Anyone visiting Russia will be dealing with several branches and activities of this organization which controls every aspect of tourism in Russia from giving you its brochures to granting you a visa to booking a room in one of the hotels, and finally bidding you farewell as you purchase your last souvenir from the airport duty-free Beriozka shop.

Intourist was established in 1929 and by 1966 had handled its first million tourists. According to its own statistics it maintains contacts with 700 foreign travel and transport agencies and has offices in 29 countries world-wide. At home its guides speak a total of 30 languages and they with their tour buses or limousines, provide a complete tour service. As a matter of fact, although they do not advertise it there are certain areas outside of Moscow which, because of security reasons, can not be visited without an official guide. Intourist offers more than 600 intineraries within the Soviet Union.

Their offices abroad are very well organized and generally have a good supply of information. The personnel are very helpful and friendly and anyone planning to visit the Soviet Union should go or write to the nearest office listed in the telephone directory.

If your time is limited arrange through them, they can find you bookings and tickets available no other way. They will even arrange a special interest tour if none already exists.

Moscow by night

> **INFOTIP:** Moscow Intourist address is: 16 Marx Prospekt, Moscow 103099 Tel. 292-2260, telex 411211. There is another office at 1 Gorky Street.

Tours and Cruises

Believe it or not, cruises to the Soviet Union are so popular that, for some, a tour to Moscow or Leningrad is just a sideline event. Last year over seven million people choose this method of travel and many companies specialize only in cruises. These come in many variations and destinations and they come in several degrees of luxury. With its almost countless waterways (supplemented by many canals) the Soviet Union is readily accessible by ship.

The Old and the New

THE METRIC SYSTEM

Length

1 millimetre	0.04 inches
1 centimetre	0.39 inches
1 metre	1.09 yards
1 kilometre	0.62 mile

Converting kilometres to miles is as simple as multiplying the number of kilometres by 0.62.(e.g. 10km's x 0.62 6.2 miles)

Converting miles to kilometres is done by multyplying the number of miles by 1.61 (e.g. 60mi x 1.61 96.6km's)

Capacity

1 litre	33.92 ounces
	1.06 quart
0.26 gallons	

Converting litres to gallons, multiply the num'er of litres by .26. (e.g. 20l x .26 5.2 gallons)

Converting gallons to litres multiply number of gallons by 3.79. (e.g. 10 gal x 3.79 37.9l)

Weight

1 gram 0.04 ounces
1 kilogram 2.2 pounds

Converting kilograms to pounds, multiply number of kilos by 2.2. (e.g. 55 kg x 2.2 121 pounds)

Converting pounds to kilograms, multiply number of pounds by .45. (e.g. 100 pounds x .45 45 kilos)

Area

1 hectare 10000m/sqr or 2.47 acres

Converting hectares to acres, multiply the number of hectares by 2.47 (e.g. 10 ha x 2.47 24.7 acres)

Converting acres to hectares, multiply the number of acres by .41 (e.g. 40 acres x .41 16.4 ha)

Temperature

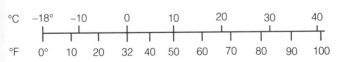

°C	−18°	−10		0		10		20		30		40	
°F	0°	10	20	32	40	50	60	70	80	90	100		

PART V
Business Guide

Pavillion of Foreign Exhibitions

BUSINESS GUIDE

Contents

General Notes

Doing business in the Soviet Union is complicated, difficult, frustrating and requires, above all, patience and persistance. Indications are that in the feature it also will be immensely rewarding. in some ways perestroika has complicated matters. For example, last September twenty ministries were supposedly abolished. In reality they have been amlgamated with others together with their personnel (bureaucrats, like soldiers, never die, they transmogrify) and now finding out who is doing what and under which telephone number is taking considerable effort.

A very pragmatic and astute young man in the Commercial Department of the British Embassy gives this advice, *'First do your home work!'* Because conditions in Russia are changing so rapidly he said he spends two months of the year updating his trade advisory 'Bible!'

British businessmen considering doing business in the Soviet Union should first study the trade possibilities in the USSR and determine whether or not his particular product or service is a viable one for that country.

> **INFOTIP:** There are many books on business currently available such as; 'Information Moscow', 'New Business USSR', Martin Walker's 'Guide to Soviet Russia', available in UK by bigger bookshops such as Hatchard's and W.H.Smith.

Your next stop should be to the local area Board of Trade to discuss the idea with them. They will give you every assistance possible. If, after all this, the idea still seems to be profitable one, contact the:

Commercial Department,
7/4 Kulluzovsky Prospekt
Moscow 121248
Tel. 214 1033 Telex 413 314

USA businessmen can contact the: **Official Soviet Trading Company AMTRAZ**, in New York or the Department of Commerce in Washington D.C., which has a Soviet desk. The US and the Soviet have a joint commission which meets once a year. There are also various working groups which meet periodically to discuss business potential.

In agreement with the British Consular Department, the Commercial Office of the US advises that '*the situation is too fluid to give precise information*'. In other words, everybody is hedging his bets! The fact is that the market in Russia is constantly changing. A ministry may suddenly obtain money to buy machinery or whatever, when for six months none was to be had. Before going to the Soviet Union the US businessman must be sponsored by a Soviet organization which is interested in his product.

US Commercial Office
Ulitsa Chaikovsovo 15
Moscow
Fax 230 2101

This office gives you a concise booklet of information compiled by the managment consulting firm of Ernst & Whinney which is also available at their offices, entitled **'Doing Business in the USSR'**. For a copy write to:

Ernst & Whinney
Bechett House
1 Lambeth Palace Road
London SE 17 EV
England

Ernst & Whinney
787 Seventh Avenue
New York 10019
U.S.A.

Capturing the USSR Market

There are two major stumbling blocks for any business, particularly small business who wish to open markets in the USSR, **a)** non-convertability of the rouble, and **b)** the time and money required to do preliminary market research. Despite this, there is a great competion among would-be enterpreneurs because of the enormous potential.

A great advange would lie with anyone able to arrange a countertrade agreement such as Pepsi did, taking their profits in vodka which they market world-wide. This type of deal is hard to come by and until the rouble is freely convertible (a projection of the Soviets for the mid-ninties) many difficulties remain. Last year, however, the Soviet Union announced the purchase of three million computers from 'the **Phoenix Group** of the **US** to be used for classrooms. The contract was obtained over 17 competitors because it offered manufacturing assistance and accepted payment not entirely in dollars.

Japan also announced the negotiation of a contract for a paper processing plant with a 200.00 ton capacity. In September 1988 Japanese firms took over the entire business hotel and trade center, **Mezhdunarodnaya**, for one month to display their wares.

This shows the imagination and aggressiveness required to capture this market. So far both the British and American governments have shown a remarkable timidity in doing business in the Soviet Union. Although the consumer market is wide open, the only products the Soviets know from USA are blue jeans and Pepsi!

The Soviets do a great deal of business at trade fairs and exhibitions, actually signing contracts on the spot. Radio Moscow News Service advertises a 'New Markets' bulletin daily.

The telex number for information concerning new enterprises is: Moscow 4111437.

Exchanging of Currency

All hotels, the airports and major train stations have facilities for exchanging money. Be sure to keep the receipts and always have your currency declaration form with you. Roubles can not be taken out of the country, but by showing these receipts they can be redeemed for foreign currency.

If possible, take American currency with you, especially in small denominations, and even coins, because they are used for change in the Beriozka stores. All foreign hard currency and combinations are accepted, but you are better off with dollars. If you have roubles left to reconvert, do so before going to the airport, there are always long lines at the currency windows.

Credit Cards

Major credit cards are eagerly accepted by hotels, restaurants, the big department stores the Beriozka shops, camping grounds and motels. All Intourist services can be paid by credit card. Roubles bought by credit card can NOT be reconverted.

Exhibitions

At any time there may be at least a dozen exhibitions scattered over Moscow ranging from displays of tractor equipment to art exhibits, book fairs and stamp shows. Intourist often arranges special tours in conjuction with them as well as special interest tours for pastors to spelunkers. Check with Intourist.

Zeal and Zest

Your trip to Russia could well be the zenith of your travels, depending on the zeal and zest with which it is undertaken.

This is a beautiful country with fascinating people and whatever inconveniences you may encounter are always forgotten in its wonders. No one could put it better than one tourist who said: *'After all, they are giving us the best they can offer'*.

St. Saviour's clock and a dome

LEGEND

━━━━━	Main Road
────────	Railway
✈	International Airport
✈	Airport

0   500   1000
Kilometres

ARCTIC

ATLANTIC
OCEAN

Svalbard

United Kingdom

BARENTS
SEA

Norway
○Oslo   Sweden

Novaya Zemlya

Stockholm○   Finland   ○Murmansk

Germany   Baltic Sea   ○Helsinki

Poland   Riga○   ○Leningrad   ○Arklangel'sk

Warsaw○   Minsk✈   ○Vologda

Kiyer○   ○MOSCOW   **UNION OF SOVIE**

Rumania   Khar'kov○   Kazan○

○Odessa   Saratov○   Sverdlovsk○

Rostov○   Kuybyshev○   Chelyabinsk✈   ○Omsk

Black Sea   ○Volgograd✈   Novosibirs

○Ankara

Turkey   Tbilisi○   Karaganda○✈

Baku○   Caspian Sea   ○Kzyl Orda

Syria   ○Alma Ata

Baghdad○   Tashkent✈   ○

Iraq   Tehřan○

Iran   Kabul○

Saudi Arabia   The Gulf   **Afghanistan**   India

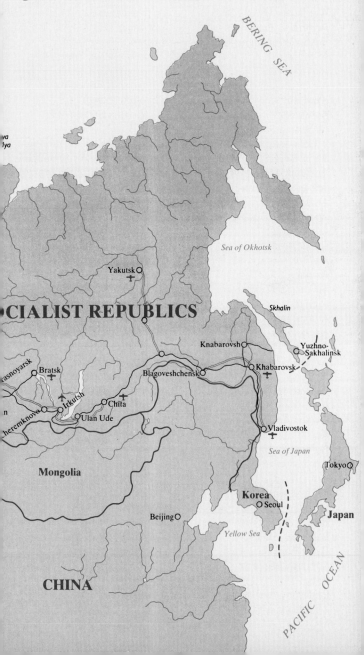

OCEAN

BERING SEA

Sea of Okhotsk

Yakutsk

CIALIST REPUBLICS

Skhalin

Krasnoyarsk
Bratsk

Knabarovsh

Yuzhno-
Sakhalinsk

Blagoveshchensk

Khabarovsk

Irkutsk
Chita

heremknova
Ulan Ude

Vladivostok

Sea of Japan

Mongolia

Tokyo

Korea
Seoul

Japan

Beijing

Yellow Sea

CHINA

PACIFIC OCEAN

Index

Alphabetical Index

Index

Index

Notes

Notes